IF MEN HAVE ALL THE POWER HOW COME WOMEN MAKE THE RULES

and other radical thoughts for men who want more fairness from women

by Jack Kammer

© 2002 Jack Kammer
some images © 2002 arttoday.com

cover design by Lou Peddicord

Healthy Village Press enriches lives
around the world by reminding human societies
of the importance and inherent worth
of men and boys and how they contribute
to healthy families, communities, towns, cities,
nations and planets.

Also by Jack Kammer

Good Will Toward Men:
Women Talk Candidly About the Balance
of Power Between the Sexes

Heroes of the Blue Sky Rebellion:
How You and Other Young Men Can Claim
All the Happiness in the World

Healthy Village Press
P.O. Box 18236
Halethorpe MD 21227 USA
information@healthyvillagepress.com
www.healthyvillagepress.com

Thanks to many progressive men and women around the world.
Especially Maria.

> "While there's much truth at the heart of this, I didn't particularly like the one-liner approach, and the contempt this book would inspire among the women in house would be immense. I'll let one of my male competitors be the one who gets pummeled."
>
> —Rick Horgan, VP & Executive Editor of Warner Books, Inc.
> *in a March 19, 1998 letter to the author's agent concerning the first edition of this book, for which we never could find a publisher*

Which pretty well proves the point, doesn't it?

Contents

The Rules 1
The Rulers 3
Foreword Not Written by Dave Barry 4
Introduction 5
Opening Thoughts 7
Debunking the Idea That Men Have All the Power 9
Identifying and Describing Female Power 18
    The Foundation of Female Power: Women's Superiority Complex 20
    Adjusting Our Eyes to See Female Power 29
    The Power of Emotions 36
    The Power of Shame 38
    The Power of Sex 50
    Women's "High-Volume Sexual Harassment" 58
    The Power of Defining the Terms 64
    Spin Control, Controlling the Agenda 67
    Feminacentrism 72
    Double Standards 79
    Debunking the Notion of Female Superiority 89

Contents

Asserting Our Own Agenda on Our Terms 104
   Taking Equal Control of Dating 104
   A Hard Man is Good to Find 112
   Equal Options for Men in Jobs and Money 114
   Equal Options for Men in Marriage and Parenting 130
   Treatment of Fathers in Divorce 146
   Domestic Violence Bigotry: The Maternalist Backlash 153
   "Herjury": False Allegations of Sexual Misconduct 157
   Abuse Abuse: "That devil made me do it." 164
   Choice for Men 166
   Suicide 169
   Saying What We Want to Say When and How We Want to Say It 173
   The "Sensitive" Man 178
   The Straightforward Man 180
   Twenty-one Points for Women Who Want Their Men to "Open Up" 186

Ending Our Collusion in Women's Unfairness 190

Statistics, "Studies," "Reports" and Other Smokescreens 197

Lexicon 205

Conclusion 207

About the Author 209

The Rules
a fax dated April 14, 1997 and posted on a woman's office wall in Washington DC

- The female always makes The Rules.
- The Rules are subject to change at any time without prior notification.
- No male can possibly know all The Rules.
- If the female suspects the male knows all The Rules, she must immediately change some or all of The Rules.
- The female is NEVER wrong.
- If the female is wrong, it is due to a misunderstanding which was a direct result of something the male did or said wrong.
- The male must apologize immediately for causing said misunderstanding.
- The female may change her mind at any time.
- The male must never change his mind without the express written consent of the female.
- The female has every right to be angry or upset at any time.
- The male must remain calm at all times unless the female wants him to be angry and/or upset.
- The female must under no circumstances let the male know whether or not she wants him to be angry and/or upset.
- The male is expected to mind read at all times.
- The female is ready when she is ready.
- The male must be ready at all times.
- Any attempt to document The Rules could result in bodily harm.
- The male who doesn't abide by The Rules lacks backbone and is a wimp.

The Rules
from *The Rules*, a book by Ellen Fein and Sherrie Schneider about
how to manipulate men into marriage, a bestseller in the USA 1995-1997

"Early on in a relationship, the man is the adversary."

"Invariably, we find that men who insist that their dates meet them halfway… turn out to be turds."

"You will probably feel cruel when you do The Rules. You will think you are making men suffer, but in reality you are actually doing them a favor… They get to experience longing!"

"[The woman] doesn't have to do anything more on the date than show up… don't make it easy for him… he has to do all the work."

"It's nice of you to care about his finances, but remember he is deriving great pleasure from taking you out."

"It's good when men get upset."

"Let him be the one to worry about the future."

The Rulers
described by Olivette Orme in the *Wall Street Journal*, May 9, 1997

The Sisterhood... dictates that in the battle between the sexes, women friends stick by each other. Men know that when the Sisterhood unites, there will be no peace until they've given up, given in or apologized and promised never to do it again.

The Rulers
described by Esther Vilar in her 1972 book *The Manipulated Man*

Women invent rules, manipulate men to obey them, and in this way dominate men—but in no way apply the rules to themselves.

Foreword Not Written by Dave Barry

Don't let the title fool you. This book is not—and is not meant to be—funny.
It's meant to be succinct.

If you want to yuk it up about men's much-discussed foibles (we're "afraid" of commitment, we never ask for directions, we cling to the remote control because it makes us feel potent, and other time-worn chestnuts women love for making them feel superior), there are plenty of other books (and newspaper columns and sitcoms) that will let you do just that.

As trite and mindlessly popular as those things are, they have the sad effect—if not the intention—of convincing us either 1) our problems with women are no big deal and should just be laughed off, 2) the problems are all our fault anyway and could be fixed easily if only we weren't so, well… male, and 3) there's nothing we can do about the problems even if we wanted to because women are just so much stronger, smarter and wiser than we are.

No, this book is about the seldom-discussed things *women* think and say and do, how they create problems for us, and how we can view those problems in a new way so we can begin to solve them.

Except for occasional instances of sarcasm and satire about women, this book is not much to laugh about. But it might make you smile in other ways.

As Dave Barry so often says, I am not making this up.

INTRODUCTION

Though some women[1] will like it a lot—just as some men appreciated the "radical" works women were writing thirty years ago—this book is for men. Most women will hate it.[*]

Why? Because it talks about female power.

Women like to pretend they have no power so they can't be held accountable for how they use it. They call us misogynists, women-haters, when we challenge their game.

Isn't it strange there isn't a widely used fifty-cent word for people who hate men?

Some will say this book is a male backlash against women, like a White Power movement against African-Americans. But in America, at least, there are no deep cultural traditions favoring blacks. There are, however, plenty favoring females. So, unlike what needs to happen in race relations, equalizing the situation between the sexes needs to be a two-way street. Denying that is a backlash against the truth.

You might hear that this book is an example of the victimhood mentality. Certainly,

---

[1] This book is written for and to men and I have made no effort to make it appealing to women, but I offer my apologies to these good women for the generalizations in this brief and purposefully pithy book. I thank you for being exceptions to what I have found to be all too common among the women of our time.

[*] That was my prediction when I released the first edition of *If Men Have...* on the Internet in October 1999. I still believe it is accurate for most women. But the average response from the women who read the first edition of the book has been positive: 6.9 on a 10-point scale. (1 = "Hated it." 10 = "Loved it.") (The average rating from men is 8.9.)

denying personal responsibility is unhealthy. But so is the opposite: pretending everything is just fine when it isn't. That's the unhealthy behavior we men tend to exhibit. Sometimes the most responsible thing a person can do is recognize and acknowledge he cannot handle a problem by himself, and help motivate and organize all parties involved to fix it.

It is clear that fairness to women is a lot higher priority among men than fairness to men is among women. That has to change. We have to make it change.

OPENING THOUGHTS

➢ The most curious sexism in the world is women's belief that only one sex is sexist.

➢ It is exactly because men are fair that we've listened so patiently to women's allegations that we're not.

➢ How come men never say, "It's a man's world"?

➢ Our greatest weakness is our facade of strength. Women's greatest strength is their facade of weakness.[†]

[†] Thanks to Lawrence Diggs. Similarly, philosopher Immanuel Kant noted, "Feminine traits are called weaknesses. People joke about them; fools ridicule them; but reasonable persons see very well that those traits are just the tools for the management of men, and for the use of men for female designs." [*Anthropology from a Pragmatic Point of View*, Southern Illinois University Press 1978, originally published in 1798.]

➢ The fact that we have never spoken up is either evidence that everything is okay for us… or the perfect proof of just how bad things really are.

───

➢ If men have all the power how come women make the rules?

───

Debunking the Idea that Men Have All the Power

You probably don't feel particularly powerful. We need to overcome the sexist notion that because we're men we always get what we want.

➢ If it's wrong to say women are airheads because not all women are airheads, and if it's wrong to say Blacks are criminals because not all Blacks commit crime, why is it correct to say men rule the world? Most men don't.

➢ The best way to prove that Congress is not interested in what's good for men is to imagine the furor over a Congressional candidate who says he is.

➤ If Congress is an assembly of men looking out for men, why is it focused on a supposed "crisis in women's health" and totally ignoring the fact that we die six years younger than women?

Some say the reason men die younger is that we have a Y chromosome and the situation can't be helped. It is inconceivable that anyone could be so cold as to say the reason women get breast cancer is that they have breasts and there's nothing to be done about it.

> In Fiscal Year 2000, the federal government funded research into breast cancer—which kills about 41,500 women per year—at $424,900,000. Research into prostate cancer—which kills about 31,700 men annually—got $190,000,000. In the same budget, breast cancer outreach and screening programs got $185,000,000, while such programs aimed at prostate cancer received $11,000,000.
> That's $14,700 per female death, $6340 per male.
> On February 14, 2001 Representative Randy (Duke) Cunningham (R-CA) introduced legislation to establish an Office of Men's Health to parallel the Office of Women's Health, which was created in 1991. Sixteen months after introduction the bill has not passed
> *derived from information provided by the Men's Health Network, Washington DC*

➢ Looking at men in business and government and saying we have all the power is like looking at women in the supermarket and saying they have all the food.

Women in supermarkets use their food for the benefit of those they love. They aren't thinking of what they themselves want, but rather what the kids like and what the husband needs for his cholesterol problem. Similarly, men in positions of male power don't think of themselves, but rather how they can take care of their loved ones. They hardly ever think of other men.

➢ It may be true that powerful men take care of their buddies, but powerful men are far more likely to devote their power to help and protect women they don't know than men they don't know, and most men are complete strangers to the men in power.

➢ Thinking that men in Congress care about making things better for men is like thinking Betty Crocker was a pioneer of feminism. Like Betty, congressmen are happy and content in their traditional places, wondering whatever could the problem be.

➢ A chauffeur has the keys to a powerful machine, he has an impressive uniform, and he might even choose what route to take, but he isn't the one who decides where or when to travel. The men in government drive Miss Daisy wherever she wants to go.

> "The feminists are the one constituency that President Clinton has not been willing to ruffle at all."
> —*Cokie Roberts, NPR "Morning Edition," May 19, 1997.*

Examples of powerful men's tendency to automatically, unthinkingly and often stupidly rush to women's aid

"Senate Majority Leader Trent Lott charged the Air Force with abusing [Kelly] Flinn [a female Air Force pilot facing court-martial for lying, disobeying orders and adultery], saying she should be granted an honorable discharge…

"[Sen. Tom] Harkin pressed on, asking [Air Force Chief of Staff, General Ronald] Fogleman why the young aviator was being charged with adultery and not with lying and disobeying an order.

"'She is!' said Fogleman, to which Harkin replied: 'I thought she was just charged with adultery.'"

—*Associated Press, May 21, 1997*

"'My wife has a good question,' said Lott… 'Where's the guy who's involved in this deal?'"

—*New York Times, May 21, 1997*

(The "guy" was a civilian and was, of course, not charged with disobeying orders or lying to superiors.)

**Examples of powerful women's willingness
to go to war for other women no matter what**

A group of female members of Congress, including Republicans as well as Democrats, insisted that the Air Force should grant Kelly Flinn the honorable discharge she wanted, even though Flinn admitted she had an affair with a civilian, lied to Air Force investigators about it and disobeyed an order from her commanding officer that she stay away from the man. The female House members portrayed Flinn as a "trailblazer" who should suffer no repercussions for her wrongdoing. Rep. Nancy L. Johnson (R-CT) said, "She has by every measure performed to the highest standards as a pilot and complied with the military code of conduct rigorously in her professional activities."

derived from the Washington Post, *May 22, 1997*

*Flinn was allowed to resign from the Air Force with an
uncharacterized discharge rather than face court martial.
An uncharacterized discharge is officially neither honorable nor dishonorable.*

Women are more valuable than we are. That must be what they mean.

"I personally don't think women should be in combat, but that's a personal view based on my feeling that women are too valuable to be in combat."

—*former Defense Secretary Caspar Weinberger*
"This Week," ABC News, June 8, 1997

• • •

The *Washington Times*, in an editorial on May 31, 2002, said that an Army decision to staff Reconnaissance, Surveillance and Target Acquisition units only with men is "welcome news—because it means less chance that female soldiers will be killed or wounded by enemy fire."

Fewer women will die. More men will die. What's welcome about that?

Judges and juries also operate on the notion that women are more valuable.

Drunk drivers who kill women get prison sentences that are 56 per cent longer than the sentences given to drunk drivers who kill men.

derived from National Bureau of Economic Research at Harvard University, April 2000

> **And of course the media are famous for insinuating that men are unworthy of concern**
>
> As far into our supposedly progressive millennium as July 1, 2002 a news organization as supposedly enlightened as the USA's National Public Radio gave an early report of an errant American bomb that killed Afghan civilians attending a wedding. In describing the victims, NPR used the phrase "including women and children," apparently to emphasize the horror of the mishap. We can certainly understand the special sadness caused by the death of youngsters, but one wonders whether the obliteration of a bachelor party would have made the news at all.
>
> Be aware also that when the media tell of victims and "a majority are women and children," it is often likely true that "a majority are men and children" as well.

➢ Would the Senate be more balanced on gender issues than it is now if it had fifty typical women senators and fifty of the most pro-male senators you can name? Can you name even one pro-male senator?

> "In my house, being raised with a sister and three brothers, there was an absolute—a nuclear—sanction if under any circumstances, for any reason, no matter how justified—even self-defense—if you ever touched our sister, literally, not figuratively, literally. My sister, who's my best friend, my campaign manager, my confidante, grew up with absolute impunity in our household… and I have the bruises to prove it. And I mean that sincerely. I'm not exaggerating when I say that."
>
> *—Senator Joseph Biden*
> *during Senate Judiciary Committee Hearings*
> *on his bill to protect women, but not men, from violence*
> *December 11, 1990*

IDENTIFYING AND DESCRIBING FEMALE POWER

> Tom: Women don't know how much power they have. Or do they?
> Ray: Sssshhhh!
> *Tom and Ray Magliozzi on an archived edition of NPR's "Car Talk" broadcast on WAMU-FM in Washington, June 8, 2002*
>
> *Did Ray want Tom to be quiet because he doesn't think women know how much power they have and doesn't want them to know, or because he knows women don't like men talking about their power? Either way, it's pretty telling that the topic of female power is taboo.*

Women's power is difficult to see and measure. But we better get a grip on it. As long as women can pretend they don't have any power, we can't call them on how they use—and misuse—it. And they get to keep what they have all to themselves.

- Pheminism[2] taught us that no one gives up power willingly. Especially not pheminists.

- We know female power exists because women are not our slaves. They must be using something quite potent to counteract all the terrible powers and tendencies women themselves say we have.

- What is the power that gives a 115-pound woman the audacity to jump in the face and give endless grief to a 220-pound man, when no 115-pound man would dare to do the same?

- It's tough to trust a person who holds a club behind her back and says, "A club? What club? I don't have a club."

---

[2] A term combining "phony" and "feminism" to denote the wrongheaded idea that "equal rights for women" is the same thing as "more and special rights for women."

The Foundation of Female Power: Women's Superiority Complex

Though they deny it as much as they can, women know they have a lot of power over us. One way they rationalize it is by believing they're better than we are. Since women think they're better, they think they have the right—even the sacred duty—to keep us under their control.

The women's movement has helped men examine our attitudes of superiority over women. Now women need to look at how they think they're superior to us.

The idea of Female Superiority goes way back. Dr. John Gordon, a professor of English at Connecticut College, says that in the 1800s anti-male novels and anti-male tracts—thousands of them—"were part of a campaign to represent men as barbarians whose urges had to be leashed in by the forces of decency—meaning women—if civilization were to survive."

> "It is an amazing thing to see in our city the wife of a shoemaker, or a butcher, or a porter dressed in silk with chains of gold at the throat, with pearls and a ring of good value… and then in contrast to see her husband cutting the meat, all smeared with cow's blood, poorly dressed, or burdened like an ass, clothed with the stuff from which sacks are made… but whoever considers this carefully will find it reasonable, because it is necessary that the lady, even if low-born and humble, be draped with such clothes for her natural excellence and dignity, and that the man [be] less adorned as if a slave, or a little ass, born to her service."
>
> —*Lucrezia Marinella of Venice, Italy, 1600*
> The Nobility and Excellence of Women Together
> With the Defects and Deficiencies of Men

What's wrong with this picture?

"When will you need it?" Red Zone Anti-Perspirant Ad, Spin Magazine, February 2001

(Is that Lucrezia Marinella riding in the car?)

"I married beneath me. All women do."

—*Lady Nancy Astor (1879–1964)*

"I believe that women have a capacity for understanding and compassion which a man structurally does not have, does not have it because he cannot have it. He's just incapable of it."

—*Barbara Jordan, former member of the US Congress from Texas, speaking to the Women's Campaign Research Fund, Austin, Texas, September 1991*

"Among the low-income couples we observed, the battle between the sexes often looks more like outright war, and many women say that they regard men simply as 'children,' 'no good,' or 'low-down dirty dogs.'"

—*Researcher Kathryn Edin, as reported in* The American Prospect, *January 3, 2000*

"A boy is to be a boy, and then becomes a man… He is taught to respect females as a higher category of mortal being."

—*Karen De Coster, writing in LewRockwell.com August 14, 2001*

The inside of this best-selling card from Hallmark says, "Excuse me. For a second there, I was feeling generous."

Incredibly, Hallmark's web site says, "We create products that help people capture their emotions and share them with one another… We strive to offer people a rich array of vivid and memorable ways to express their feelings, and their countless relationships, all over the world. Yet within this diversity, we seek, always, to honor and serve what is universal to the human heart: the need to love and be loved, to be understood and to understand, to sustain hope, to celebrate, to laugh, to heal. We are in a rare business: we help to bring people together, make them happy, and give them ways to show how much they care."

As long as women get away with thinking we're inferior, they'll have no qualms about treating us badly. They might not even know they're doing it.

> "Women's protectiveness is inherently condescending, a sisterly solidarity that says, 'We know better. We must look after these children we have married.'"
> —*therapist Terrence Real in his 1997 book* I Don't Want to Talk About It: Overcoming the Secret Legacy of Male Depression

➢ Any man would be damaged by the allegation that "he doesn't respect women." Why is it so hard to imagine that any woman would be hurt by the charge that "she doesn't respect men"?

> "What bothers me most is the visible, although often unspoken, thread of contempt that runs through women's conversations about men. The assumption very often is that men are boys who must be outfoxed, manipulated or dealt with in a calculated manner that women rarely use among themselves."
> —*Phyllis Theroux in* GQ, *February 1986*
>
> "Looking at how easy it is for women to treat men in cruel ways is oddly liberating."
> —*Naomi Wolf in her 1993 book* Fire With Fire

Women get a lot of power just out of the fact that they expect and demand special and preferential treatment.

Women Demand Too Much! (Or Do We Demand Too Little?)

American women think government officials don't pay enough attention to women's health issues, according to a survey. "Women want their healthcare concerns considered and given greater priority in Washington and in the state capitals,'" the survey director said. "And women were a major force in the 2000 elections."

derived from Reuters Health, November 16, 2001

Average Life Expectancy at Birth, Year 2000

Males: 74.1 years   Females: 79.5 years

—*US National Vital Statistics Reports, Vol. 49, No. 12*

Hmmm… Could that kind of selfish "identity politics" be what made the architects of democracy reluctant to give women the vote?

> At an elementary school Reading Night in Maryland in March 2001, part of the program was a quiz game about books. The children organized themselves into two teams, girls against boys. "Who goes first?" the teacher asked. "Ladies first," some of the girls shouted. The teacher, wisely and equitably, flipped a coin. When the girls won the toss one of the girls said, "That's proper," and her friends nodded in solemn agreement.

Young men are faring poorly in school these days: they're more likely to be in special ed, more likely to be suspended, more likely to get Ritalin because of being diagnosed as hyperactive, and less likely to go to college. Educators are wondering why. Though the problem is complex, here is one important factor. High morale contributes to enhanced performance. Pep rallies boost morale. American culture for thirty years has been one unrelenting pep rally for girls. Boys have been told to sit quietly and stop causing trouble because we rooted for their team long enough. The cheers sounds a little like this. "Yea, girls. Boo, boys."

➤ If young men were being drafted and killed, and the President said that as a sign of peace all young women would wear flowers in their hair, even for just one day, women would say "Wear flowers in our hair? We will not! That's sexist!"[†]

➤ Young men are subject to the military draft in case of national military emergencies. Why aren't young women being drafted now to alleviate the day care crisis? Is one idea sexist and the other not?

➤ Imagine a migrant farm worker in a steamy bunkhouse with a broken fan. Imagine a guest in a luxury hotel whose air conditioning isn't working just right. Who is more likely to complain? Who has more to complain about?

Sometimes a complaint tells us more about the expectations of the complainer than the actual circumstances the complainer is in.

[†] Thanks to Fred Hayward, director of MR, Inc.

Adjusting Our Eyes to See Female Power

➤ There are two possible reasons why we keep hearing that we live in a patriarchy. The first is that we do indeed live in a society dominated by men. The other possibility is that we live under a different kind of rule that is so strong and so pervasive that it keeps us from seeing it for what it is.

> "Cherokee women didn't have titled positions. The men had those. But women had the Women's Council. They had a lot of control. People forget that... With the Iroquois the chief was a man, but the women chose the chief, they nurtured him, they installed him. Women could take him out."
> —*Wilma Mankiller, principal chief of the Cherokee Nation, 1987-1995, speaking at the University of Arizona in January 2002, as broadcast on C-SPAN, June 1, 2002*

➢ Women's power is the opposite of monumental. It's like wall-to-wall carpeting, or a snowfall, everywhere and unavoidable, not concentrated into a few narrow, vertical monuments, like men's.

> Phyllis Schlafly gets a big kick out of the story of a hoodwinked husband boasting foolishly to his friends: "When my wife and I were married, we agreed that I would make all the major decisions, and she would make the minor ones. I decide what legislation Congress should pass, what treaties the president should sign, and whether the United States should stay in the United Nations. My wife makes the minor decisions—such as how we spend our money, whether I should change my job, where we should live, and where we go on our vacations."
> —*from Schlafly's 1977 book* The Power of the Positive Woman

➢ Women get away with more bad behavior than we do because our mischief tends to rise abruptly for all the world to see. Women's mischief often hugs the terrain like a low-level bomber invisible to radar.

As a new seventh-grade teacher in Winslow, Arizona in 1974, I drew two graphs on the chalkboard. Pointing to the graph on the left I said, "This is how a boy is typically bad. He throws an eraser, laughs out loud, or yells. He isn't bad for very long, but when he's bad there's no denying it." I turned to the other graph. "This is how a girl is typically bad. At any moment she's only doing little things like whispering or giggling, but she does it for a much longer time."

"The shaded area," I said, "shows that the total 'badness' is about the same. Boys who misbehave in my class will be punished as I'm sure they always have been. But if I should punish a girl for something much less obvious than throwing an eraser, don't complain that you weren't doing much. Consider instead how long you were doing it." Naturally enough the boys were happy with this enlightened standard of justice and discipline. But to my delight, the girls, too, liked the fact that somebody had called them on their game.

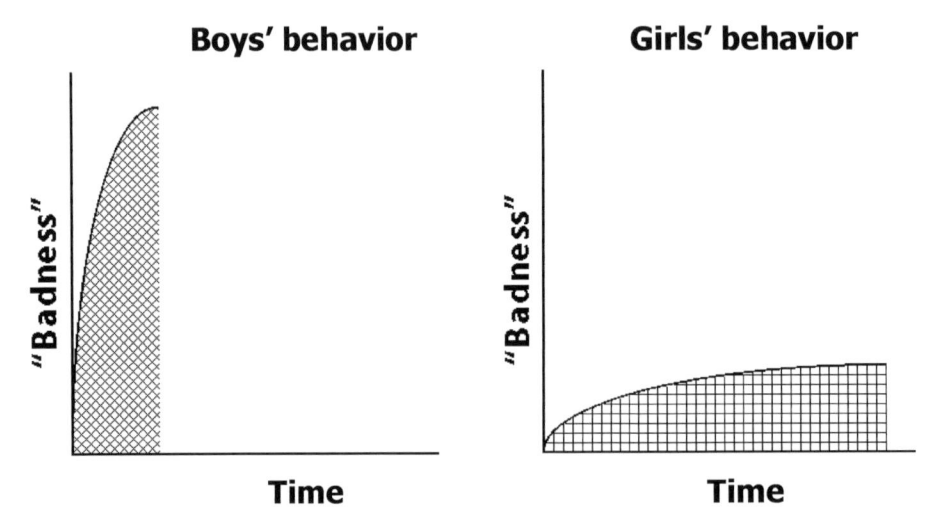

> "In studying female aggression, Dr. [Wendy] Craig [a professor of developmental psychology at Queen's University in Kingston, Ontario] found that girls are just as aggressive as boys. Unlike male aggression, which is physical, female social aggression is covert and, therefore, hard to detect. 'Girl aggression tends to be social in nature—that is, emotionally rejecting, dismissive, and verbally abusive,' she says. 'This kind of aggression has as many negative consequences as physical aggression. The victims of social aggression become anxious, depressed, fearful, and have a lower self-concept.' The implication is that, as future parents, socially aggressive females have the potential to inflict great harm, which can go undetected by society."
> —*Queen's University press release, March 18, 1997*

> "[Women] bully in more or less the same way [as men] with the exception that females are actually much better at it, they're much more devious, much more manipulative, much more subtle about it and they leave a lot less evidence as well—and they can often do it with a smile."
> —*Tim Field, who established Britain's National Workplace Bullying Line in 1996, reported in* The Australian, *July 12, 1999*

"[T]he central organizing principle of primate social life is competition between females and especially female lineages… Females should be, if anything, more competitive than males, not less, although the manner in which females compete may be less direct, less boisterous, and hence more difficult to measure… We are not yet equipped to measure the elaborations upon old themes that our fabulously inventive, and devious, species creates daily."

—*Sarah Blaffer Hrdy, Ph.D.*
in her 1981 book The Woman That Never Evolved

"Most of the damage women do is indirect. If she only bats her eyes to induce a guy into a fight, nobody's going to blame her. Women do a lot of things that provoke and trigger responses in men. But nobody seems able to see that."

—*Herb Goldberg, Ph.D.*
author of The Hazards of Being Male
in an interview with Jack Kammer, December 2, 1990

Recently I had a conversation with a group of women in which I said that women generally seem to do a much better job of sticking together than men do. I wasn't asking for a reason or a cause. I wanted to talk about the effect. But the women didn't want to talk about that. They immediately got defensive and threw out a reason, almost like a roadblock. The reason that women stick together, they said, was "because we have to."

The clear implication was that if women don't stick together we bad and powerful men will take advantage of them since they're so good and powerless. By pretending to be powerless and by pretending to act only in reaction to what we do to them, women irresponsibly free themselves to do whatever they want to us and not feel bad about the offenses they commit.

We have to stop allowing them to pretend to be powerless. We have to insist they talk about effects as well as causes, and about causes other than the ones they want us to accept.

The Power of Emotions

➤ Computer hardware looks impressive. Software doesn't look like much. But anyone who understands computing knows that the power is in the programming.

➤ When it comes to emotions, we're like ditzy women who think they can't balance a checkbook, like utterly dependent females who run to men for their weekly allowance. We let women handle our emotions for us. That gives them a lot of control.

> "A contemporary man often assumes that a woman knows more about a relationship than he does, allows a woman's moods to run the house, assumes that when she attacks him, she is doing it 'for his own good.'"
>
> —*poet Robert Bly*
> *in his 1990 book* Iron John

> "Psychologically speaking, nine out of 10 women will take nine out of 10 men in a fight to the finish, not with direct, head-on aggression, but with guilt, shame and blame... As men we need to learn how not to be vulnerable to women when we shouldn't be."
>
> —*philosopher Sam Keen*
> *author of* Fire in The Belly

The Power of Shame

> "One of the most effective ways I have seen women using to gain power over men is by shaming men, using their tongue to put men down, to shame their sexuality, to shame their success."
>
> —*Char Tosi, founder of Woman Within* in Good Will Toward Men *by Jack Kammer*

**A story about men
and domestic violence**

The Super Bowl is a big event enjoyed by millions of people every year, most of them male.

The game typifies the hopes and dreams of many American males. It glorifies everything lots of boys and men want to be: strong, fast, big, tough and adored by huge crowds.

**A story about women
and child abuse**

The Miss America Pageant is a big event enjoyed by millions of people every year, most of them female.

The beauty contest typifies the hopes and dreams of many American females. It glorifies everything lots of girls and women want to be: slim, beautiful, talented and adored by huge crowds.

If Men Have All the Power How Come Women Make the Rules

But the dirty little secret of the Super Bowl is that it causes men to commit domestic violence.

Experts, in fact, have identified Super Bowl Sunday as a Day of Dread for American Women.

At a press conference near the stadium, a group of people concerned with women's rights pronounced Super Bowl Sunday "the biggest day of the year for violence against women."

If the man's team is losing, or if they fumble the ball, the man's pent-up anxiety often explodes into violence against his wife.

If a woman dares to speak or otherwise distract a man during the Super Bowl, the man will often go berserk and strike her for insolence and disrespect.

But the dirty little secret of the Miss America Pageant is that it causes women to commit child abuse.

Experts, in fact, have identified Miss America Saturday as a Day of Dread for American Children.

At a press conference in Atlantic City, a group of people concerned with children's welfare pronounced Miss America Saturday "the biggest day of the year for violence against children."

If the woman's favorite contestant is eliminated, or if she fumbles a question, the woman's pent-up anxiety often explodes into violence against her kids.

If a child dares to speak or otherwise distract a woman during the Miss America contest, the woman will often go berserk and strike the child for insolence and disrespect.

No one can explain exactly why, but some say that the game puts men face-to-face with the frustrations and disappointments of their lives. When men look at their wives during the Super Bowl, they feel anger and rage toward their spouses for making them be something other than football stars.

The real explanation, however, is obvious enough. Though no one can prove it, the evidence seems strong that during the game men's testosterone surges and, well, we all know what testosterone does.

Moreover, it is common knowledge that men take it as their traditional right to beat women. In fact, the term "Rule of Thumb" came from the old law that said a man could beat his wife as long as he used a stick no thicker than his thumb.

To help stem the horrible tide of violence against women, NBC has agreed to air a Public Service Announcement right before the game. It will be directed squarely at men and will remind them just as they are settling in for their big event that "domestic violence is a crime."

No one can explain exactly why but some say that the pageant puts women face-to-face with the frustrations and disappointments of their lives. When women look at their children during the Miss America contest, they feel anger and rage toward their kids for making them be something other than beauty queens.

The real explanation, however, is obvious enough. Though no one can prove it, the evidence seems strong that during the pageant women experience a form of PMS and, well, we all know what PMS does.

Moreover, it is common knowledge that women take it as their traditional right to beat children. In fact, the term "Rule of Thumb" came from the old law that said a woman could beat her children as long as she used a stick no thicker than the child's thumb.

To help stem the horrible tide of violence against children, ABC has agreed to air a Public Service Announcement right before the pageant. It will be directed squarely at women and will remind them just as they are settling in for their big event that "child abuse is a crime."

On "Good Morning America" a renowned psychologist reinforced the warning about the dangers of Super Bowl Sunday, claiming to have ten years of domestic violence statistics to prove her point.

The *Boston Globe*, one of the nation's most respected newspapers, ran a story saying that domestic violence hot lines and shelters are "flooded with more calls from victims [on Super Bowl Sunday] than any day of the year."

Activists mailed a notice to women, warning them: "Don't remain alone with him during the game."

This really happened.

On the "Today Show" a renowned psychologist reinforced the warning about the dangers of Miss America Saturday, claiming to have ten years of child abuse statistics to prove his point.

The *Boston Globe*, one of the nation's most respected newspapers ran, a story saying that child abuse hot lines and child protection agencies are "flooded with more calls from victims [on Miss America Saturday] than any day of the year."

Activists mailed a notice to fathers, warning them: "Don't let the children remain alone with her during the pageant."

Nothing like this ever happened.

The Miss America story is completely fictitious. But if it had happened, what would you think? You might think that it's good to protect children from abuse, right? But what if it later turned out that the whole story about child abuse surging during the Miss America Pageant was one huge, bald-faced lie? What would you think then? Would it not seem that some organization or some ideology with a lot of power and influence wanted cruelly and arrogantly to spray shame all over one of the events millions of American women enjoy most? Would it not seem that someone wanted unjustifiably to shame certain ideals of American femininity and even to shame American women themselves?

On the other hand, the Super Bowl story really did happen. Fortunately, Ken Ringle, an enterprising reporter for the *Washington Post*, found that it was all a lie, that all the statistics and claims and "science" were bogus, that there is no evidence that domestic violence increases during the Super Bowl. (Unfortunately, you'll still hear that it does, but you can confidently refute the claim and refuse the shame.) Ringle's article appeared in the *Washington Post* on Super Bowl Sunday, January 31, 1993.

Shaming maleness and masculinity around domestic violence is the key tactic in the backlash against men, which we'll talk about later.

➢ Boys grow up learning they're not sugar, not spice, not anything nice.

> "A [15-year-old male New Zealand high school] student has been [suspended] for five days [the maximum] for writing an essay considered sexually offensive. [He] had to write a story in his year 10 English class titled: How does your body betray you? He wrote about an embarrassed teenager whom he described as having 'a boner' (an erection), while in class and not wanting to leave his seat when called to the front of the class. His [female] English teacher showed the story to [the female] principal… who said it was 'sexually offensive' and 'totally inappropriate.'"
> —Sunday Star Times, *Auckland, New Zealand*
> *May 12, 2002*

➤ In western culture we picture women right below the angels, and men just above the animals.

These signs were erected in Manhattan with permission, tools and equipment provided by the City of New York.

➤ Women's whole tired toilet seat harangue is all about shame and control. What would you think of a man who got haughty and belittling every time his wife failed to return the driver's seat to his preferred position after she finished using the family car?

Testosterone: Not a thing to be ashamed of

➢ When you hear women joking that men suffer from "Testosterone Poisoning," remind them that similarly shallow and sexist ideas led the ancient Greeks to coin the term "hysteria" from their word for the uterus.

> "For every male-related hormonal or genetic problem, you can find a female parallel. Pre-Menstrual Syndrome or menopause, for example. So I don't know that anybody has actually tried to come up with an accurate rating of which gender's hormones cause the most havoc."
> —*Suzanne Steinmetz, Ph.D., sociologist and violence researcher
> in* Good Will Toward Men *by Jack Kammer*

> "Testosterone may not be the dread 'hormone of aggression' that research and the popular imagination have long had it… If anything, [testosterone] may be a source of very different sensations: calmness, happiness and friendliness, for example… Researchers said that… men… who… were low in testosterone described feelings of edginess, anger, irritability, aggression… Some studies even indicate another improbable source of aggression: estrogen. Yes, the gal hormone."
> —New York Times, *June 20, 1995*

A search of the Nexis electronic database on March 29, 2001 found 94 news articles with the words "testosterone" and "poison" within two words of each other and only one story with the words "estrogen" and "poison" in the same close relationship. There were 98 news stories with "testosterone" within two words of "crazed" or "crazy." There were only three articles when the search used the word "estrogen" in place of "testosterone."

> Boys with a disorder called Kleinfelter's syndrome tend to be aggressive. They have an extra female chromosome (XXY) and have small genitals and low testosterone. Are they aggressive because they have small penises, because they have low testosterone or because of some other reason? It's hard to tell. But it's clear that they don't feel confident in their masculinity. They're aggressive yet they don't have much testosterone.
>
> Could it be that not feeling confident and secure is what causes violence?

> A 1996 study conducted at the University of Montreal and published in the *Journal of the American Academy of Child and Adolescent Psychiatry* found that thirteen-year-old boys who were most aggressive and least popular had lower levels of testosterone than the popular, genuinely tough, but not physically aggressive boys.
>
> Could it be that testosterone makes boys and men feel confident and therefore calm?

New research suggests that popular opinion has the relationship between testosterone and conflict completely backward. It appears that testosterone levels might go temporarily higher as a result of conflict, as a boost to confidence and effectiveness in an upcoming struggle, rather than as a cause of that conflict and struggle. Boys who are exposed to a lot of stress and conflict have higher levels of testosterone than they do when they are restored to a peaceful, secure environment.

> "What about the link between testosterone and aggression? Males have more testosterone circulating than females and men are more aggressive. Therefore, testosterone causes aggression: that is how this research is reported in the media… The reality is much more complicated… By concentrating on testosterone, the quintessential male hormone, those who most loudly trumpet its alleged causal role in aggression and dominance do so in support of an ideological position."
>
> —*Professor Anthony Clare from his 2000 book* On Men: Masculinity in Crisis, *quoted in the* Melbourne Sunday Herald-Sun *(Australia) October 1, 2000*

> **What's good for the gander…**
>
> "Scientists… [in Melbourne, Australia] believe that the low moods and low libido of some women are related to reduced levels of the male hormone testosterone… In a recent pilot study, [a researcher] gave testosterone supplements to 45 women aged 35 to 45 who complained of low mood and low libido and who had low testosterone levels. The therapy significantly improved the mood and well-being of more than half of them, she said."
>
> —The Age *(Melbourne), April 24, 2002*

The Power of Sex

> "There's an exquisite power to be gained in being desired."
> —Lucinda Rosenfeld, speaking of *What She Saw*, her novel about a woman's love life, Toronto Star, *October 29, 2000*

Society authorizes women to use make-up, fashion and jewelry to gain attention and stimulate sexual demand among men. "Nice girls" are not allowed to make sales calls, but they are allowed to advertise—as long as they don't cut their prices too deeply. (The Sisterhood is, among other things, a powerful trade association.)

Professor Nigel Nicholson of Reed University in Portland, Oregon teaches a class on sex and gender in ancient Rome. His class notes say "[An] aspect of sexual behavior that defined a man's masculinity was how much sex he had. Oddly, the right amount was not what we would expect; it was not very much... A large sexual appetite, whether directed at men or women or both, was considered effeminate [because] it tokened a lack of self-control, an inability to dominate oneself... " He notes a contemporary criticism of the Emperor: "Claudius enjoys sex too much, becomes overly fond of his partners, and so gives them control over him."

➢ Women laugh at us when studies show that we think about sex several times per hour. We could get a bigger laugh if anyone ever did a study of how often women think about being sexy.

➢ Why do we have trouble relating to "the powerlessness of women" whenever we see the cover of Cosmopolitan?

> "Women chat happily, send sexually explicit signals and encourage the man's attention, even if they have absolutely no interest in him. This gives a woman time to assess a man, says [Karl Grammer of the Ludwig Boltzmann Institute of Urban Ethology in Vienna, who studied 45 male-female pairs of strangers in their teens and early twenties]… Importantly, the women also seemed to control the encounter—what the women did had a direct effect on how the men behaved next. 'You can predict male behaviour from female behaviour but not the other way round,' says Grammer."
>
> —New Scientist Magazine *(London), February 14, 2001*

➤ Women say they have to control sex because we control everything else. It makes just as much sense to say that we need to control everything else because they control sex.

> "Women learn that if they're not sexual, they could be rejected. And they feel a real fear of abandonment. But they also find out that a guy will do anything to get laid. And that's pretty powerful; they control whether that man's going to get laid."
>
> —*therapist Laurie Ingraham*
> *in* Good Will Toward Men *by Jack Kammer*

➤ The army's 1996 Aberdeen sex scandal focused on sergeants who used their authority to get sex with female recruits. But what about female recruits who use their sexual power to get easier treatment from sergeants?

> "Male soldiers complained that female soldiers 'got over' on the male drill sergeants [and] fraternized with drill sergeants… to get out of training."
> —*a study by the Army Research Institute, 1995 reported in the* Washington Times, *June 5, 1997*

➤ Women's law of sexual supply and demand: keep the demand hot, keep the supply frozen.

➤ Thirty years ago, if we heard a man telling a woman during an argument that she was "cut off," we'd know he was controlling her financially. Today, when a woman tells a man he is "cut off" we know she is controlling him sexually.

> "To be blunt, sex has historically been a commodity. It's a valuable source of power… Traditionally… [a] woman's most reliable currency was the *potential* of sex… Sexual power is… the female commodity… Buried in the recesses of [women's] memories are years of messages telling us that sex is our most important asset *if* rationed, *if* kept out of reach."
> —*sex educator Carol Cassell, Ph.D. in her 1984 book* Swept Away: Why Women Fear Their Own Sexuality

The Fourth Branch of Government

"A longtime lobbyist in her fifties dresses up in 'tight leopard get-ups'… and then, essentially, lobbies with her chest, rubbing it against the appropriate arm…

"One advocate for a liberal public interest group, when interviewing for a job at a new firm, repeatedly alluded to the senators she had slept with… She apparently believed these accomplishments represented her best credentials for getting the job.

"A well-respected reporter for a major daily is known for redirecting her love interest on the Hill every time her employer switches her beat.

"One staffer, intent on marrying a congressman, has allegedly attempted to have affairs with as many of them as possible in the past few years, through expert cruising of bars and fancy receptions. Just recently she hit on Congressman Right; alas, his interest waned. Now she's threatening to expose the relationship…

"Face it, feminists: Not only is there complicity on the part of some women who walk the halls of Congress, but some see sex and sexuality as legitimate professional currency… Let's not pretend our evolution as women is complete."

—*Karen Lehrman*
Washington Post, *December 20, 1992*

➤ Erotica does not glorify our sexual domination of women. It expresses our wish that women didn't have sexual domination over us.

When we misuse our economic power over women, women legitimately react in ways we do not always like. One of those ways is to fantasize that they have achieved power over us. In the movie *9 to 5*, for instance, three women laugh merrily about how they'd like to get violent revenge against their chauvinistic male boss. In the end, the trio settles for humiliating and subduing him in a dog collar and chains.

No one could reasonably say that *9 to 5* glorifies women's domination of men in business. It is precisely because women don't dominate men in business that the fantasy is popular with women who wish they did.

Similarly, "pornography" does not glorify our sexual domination of women. It expresses our fantasies of overcoming women's sexual domination of us. The fact that *9 to 5* and some of our erotica both involve people in dog collars and chains is not mere coincidence.

What's more, some of our most popular sexual fantasies aren't about reversing sexual control at all, but are simply about equalizing it, about meeting women who participate enthusiastically in sex, who love male sexuality, and who don't hold out for money, dinner or furs. Portrayals of such egalitarian sex don't demean women any more than we are denigrated by stories of women and men working cooperatively in an office where men no longer think it is their right to have women fetch them coffee.

> "The one thing never depicted in a pornographic film is a woman criticizing her lover or demanding something different from him."
> —*therapist Terrence Real in his 1997 book* I Don't Want to Talk About It: Overcoming the Secret Legacy of Male Depression

Women's "High-Volume Sexual Harassment"

➤ If a person brings a boom box to a public street corner and plays a CD of carefully selected dance music at high volume, could he rightfully say, "Hey, stop dancing. I'm not playing this for you"?

➤ If a businessperson advertises under "Sex" in the Yellow Pages and prints the phrase "Sexy! Sexy! Sexy!" on her business cards, should she be surprised or upset when customers call her with sex on their minds?

> "If we want society to stop equating our worth with our beauty, we need to make sure that we stop it ourselves."
> —Karen Lehrman
> *in her 1997 book* The Lipstick Proviso

➤ Women need to admit their disingenuousness when they read magazines that tell them how to be sexy, buy the products that promise them they'll be sexy, use those products as directed, and then object to "unwanted" male attention by saying, "I'm not doing anything. It's your problem if you can't keep your eyes to yourself."

A product whose sole purpose is to create the illusion of erect nipples on the woman who is wearing them markets itself with a painfully phony alibi. It supposedly allows women to be "playful and perky." The product's website, however, boasts that when he first saw a woman wearing the product "a handsome Argentine stranger purred, 'For you, my paycheck… for the rest of my life.'"

➤ Criticizing women's high-volume sexual harassment does not mean women should stop being alluring to their lovers. The key issue is who else is around.

➤ If, as they claim, women dress to impress other women, not to attract men, are we supposed to believe they get breast implants to impress other women too?

To the extent that some women really do dress sexily to impress other women, the selfishness and thoughtlessness are only worse. The acid test for a heterosexual woman's sexiness—the power she is supposedly demonstrating to impress other women—is how many men she can attract or turn the heads of. Men are mere baubles, mere tally marks on a scorecard, much like the notches on the bedpost of the insincere and manipulative man whose exploitive behavior we readily see and rightly condemn, especially when his primary goal is to boast of his sexual prowess to his friends in the locker room.

It's funny we don't talk much about the Female Ego, isn't it?

➢ Women say they wear jewelry and makeup to "please" men. Yeah, and a fisherman puts a spinner on his hook to "please" the fish.

> "The mating game is powerful and primitive. There's a great deal that both sexes need to learn about that. But unfortunately right now all the blame is on men. Sexual harassment is an issue that has been controlled by women."
>
> —*Helen Fisher, Ph.D.*
> *anthropologist and author of* Anatomy of Love
> *in* Good Will Toward Men *by Jack Kammer*

Sexual harassment forces people to deal with questions of sex when they don't want to. The distraction caused by women's high-volume sexual harassment is usually at least as great as that caused by men whose sexual harassment is typically directed toward only one person.

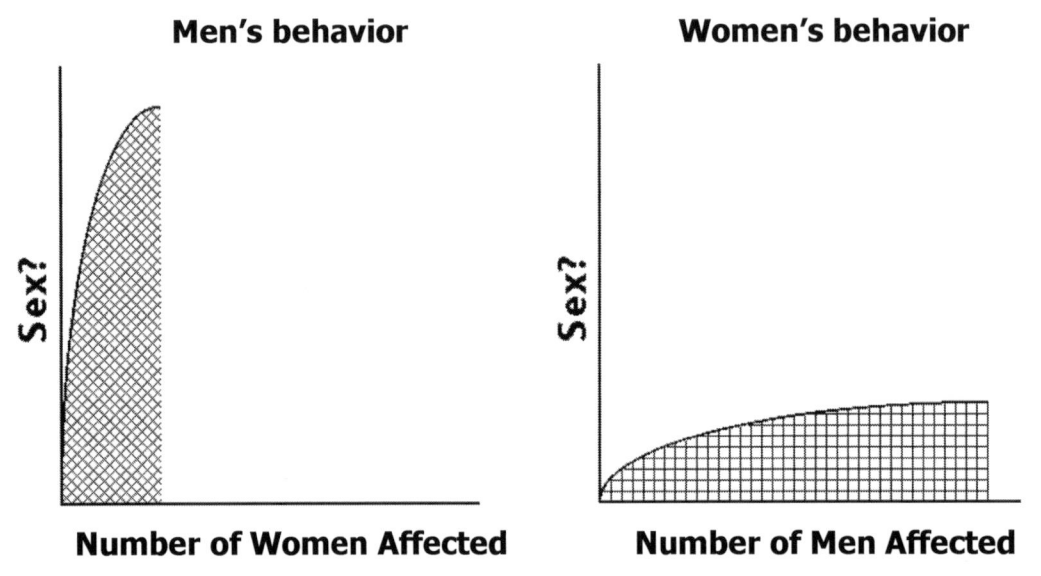

Men's behavior	**Women's behavior**
Sex? vs. Number of Women Affected	Sex? vs. Number of Men Affected

➤ Men's typical style of sexual harassment is like a pushy salesman who won't take no for an answer. Women's high-volume sexual harassment is like a junk mailer who gives you no way to get off the mailing list.

Do you ever hear a muffler-pulsing muscle car throbbing up the street and think to yourself "I'm not even going to look at that car. I don't want to encourage that rude, self-centered look-at-me noise by giving the driver the attention he so obviously wants"? I do. And I often think very much the same thing when I see a loudly decked-out, sexed-up, cleavage-popping woman walking my way. Her noise isn't the kind that you hear; it's the kind that you feel. And that only makes it worse. What would happen if millions of men and boys made a point of yawning when aggressively sex-pot women and girls walked their way?

➢ We know food that is appealing but not good for us is aptly called Junk Food. We need to develop a concept of Junk Women.

The Power of Defining the Terms

The person who defines the terms of a debate will always win.

If you let me define four as the number between five and seven, then I can argue that three plus three equals four and you'll lose the argument every time if you disagree.

> **Pheminist definitions of**
> **misogyny (woman-hating) and misandry (man-hating)**
>
> *misogyny:* "a widely accepted social attitude in a sexist world" includes beliefs that "demean [women's] bodies... abilities... characters and... efforts."
>
> *misandry:* "1) a refusal to suppress the evidence of one's experience with men; 2) a woman's defense against fear and pain; 3) an affirmation of the cathartic effects of justifiable anger."
>
> —*from A Feminist Dictionary*
> *compiled by Cheris Kramarae and Paula Treichler*

➢ Women defined sexism. And they didn't define it to refer to anything they ever think or say or do.

➤ Though Womenfirsters[3] want to define it that way, equal rights between the sexes is not always the same thing as more rights for women.

➤ Date Rape is defined in a way that can make only the man guilty. Guidelines on campuses require the man to have explicit consent prior to penetration. Why don't they require the woman to have explicit consent prior to envelopment?

➤ When women do it it's called Self-Defense or Battered Woman Syndrome. When men do it it's called Blaming the Victim and Domestic Violence—for which there is never an excuse.

Did you ever notice that overly-controlling, egotistical, micro-managing bosses always write job descriptions to describe exactly how they want the job done, even though there may be other ways just as good or even better?

---

[3] Those women and men who share a primary and overriding concern for women's interests even when they come at the expense of fairness to men and the common good.

> "Identifying love with expressing feelings is biased towards the way women prefer to behave in a love relationship."
>
> "Both scholars and the general public continue to use a feminized definition of love."
>
> "Part of the reason that men seem so much less loving than women is that men's behaviour is measured with a female ruler."
>
> —*Francesca M. Cancian in her 1987 book* Love in America: Gender and Self-Development

Spin Control, Controlling the Agenda

Womenfirsters decide what the issues are and how they are to be understood.

➤ Women want to talk about the parts of their lives in which they have a deficit, but they don't say anything about their advantages—like a shopper contesting a credit card statement without acknowledging a closet full of purchases.

➤ Womenfirsters focus attention on who earns more money and who has what jobs, but a much more important question is who lives happier, more emotionally satisfying lives. Why don't they ask that one?

➤ Womenfirsters count few women at the top of big companies and demand that we see only one possible cause: "male chauvinism." They don't count the women who have happily chosen other options.

➤ Family-friendly employment policies are getting attention now because they are affecting women. They've been affecting us for centuries without being addressed.

➤ Women make a big point that they do more of the house-cleaning than we do. But they define what's clean enough. How come you never hear a man complaining that his wife doesn't do her fair share of polishing the chrome on the Camaro?

> When in-house work and out-of-house work are totaled, men work more than women. The average American man puts in 37 hours of market labor and 16 hours of housework for a total of 53 hours per week. The average American woman works only 24 hours in the marketplace and does 27 hours of housework for a total of 51 hours per week.
> *derived from a press release from the Institute for Social Research at the University of Michigan, March 12, 2002*

A Quick Trip Through Spin City

"Three sociologists working with three different types of raw material all delivered the same fuel for making men wrong.

"The first sociologist commented on the fact that men still put in longer work weeks than women by saying that 'men are trying even harder to maintain their superiority.'

"The second sociologist saw a picture of Native American women grinding corn while the men stood watch. Her interpretation: 'the men were as usual leaving all the work to the women.'

"The third, after examining the many ways in which males, like the Indian men standing guard, took risks to protect women and children, concluded that this was another way that males maintained dominance, their own version of a 'protection racket.'

"The process is really quite simple. 'Whatever a guy does, you find a sneaky, self-serving reason.'"

—*Frank Zepezauer, writing in* The Liberator

"The Hite Report found that men prefer intercourse more than women; the American Couples survey by Schwartz and Blumstein found that women prefer intercourse more than men. Hite interpreted her findings to mean that men preferred intercourse because intercourse is male-centered, focused on penis pleasure, an outgrowth of male dominance and ego gratification. But Schwartz and Blumstein interpreted their findings in the opposite way: 'We think women prefer it because intercourse requires the equal participation of both partners more than any sexual act. Neither partner only "gives" or only "receives." Hence, women feel a shared intimacy during intercourse…' These findings are diametrically opposed, yet both interpretations could only consider the possibility that women favor intimacy and equality, and men favor ego gratification and dominance. This is distortion to fit a preconceived image."

—*Warren Farrell, Ph.D.*
author of Women Can't Hear What Men Don't Say

➢ Ask a group of friends why men initiate 75 per cent of divorces. Then ask another group why women initiate 75 per cent of divorces. You'll hear that it's men's fault either way.[†]

[†] The second statistic is correct, but that's almost irrelevant here. I conducted this experiment at Towson University, near Baltimore. Men were blamed by 88 per cent of the male students and 86 per cent of the female students who were asked to explain why men initiate 75 per cent of divorces. Of those asked to explain why women initiate 75 per cent of divorces, 25 per cent of the males and 86 per cent of the females thought that must be men's fault, too.

Feminacentrism

Feminacentrism is another manifestation of Womenfirsters' power to define the agenda. It requires looking at all problems exclusively from women's perspective, or for the purpose of seeing how women are affected. It is based on the idea that women are more virtuous, more important than men. Feminacentrism is blind to the problems men face.

**ANNOUNCING (drum roll, please)
the Winner of the Award for
The Most Incredibly Feminacentrist Statement of the Twentieth Century**

"Women have always been the primary victims of war. Women lose their husbands, their fathers, their sons in combat. Women often have to flee from the only homes they have ever known. Women are often the refugees from conflict and sometimes, more frequently in today's warfare, victims. Women are often left with the responsibility, alone, of raising the children."

—*Hillary Clinton at the First Ladies' Conference on Domestic Violence in San Salvador, El Salvador, November 17, 1998*

You dead and maimed guys are so lucky!

> **"It's not fair that you want to treat us fair!"**
>
> A feminacentrist "study" of gender bias in the Ninth Federal Judicial Circuit in 1993 asserted that gender-blind sentencing guidelines were unfair to women. "If women received lesser sentences prior to the implementation of the Guidelines, and now their sentences more closely approximate those given to men, the Guidelines would have had a disproportionately harsher effect on women than on men. In other words, while many defendants receive longer sentences under the Guidelines than previously, women's sentences may have increased more than those of men."
>
> derived from the Final Report
of the Ninth Circuit Gender Bias(ed) Task Force, note 108, page 181
>
> Suppose in the 1950s we had said that measures to equalize education between women and men were unfair to us because they increased women's schooling more than ours. Would anyone—much less a supposedly rational federal circuit court—have wasted the paper and ink to print such an argument?

Feminacentrism in the Media

For a story on August 5, 1987 reporting that 3,416 men were slain at work—82% of all at-work killings—*USA Today* used this headline: "732 women were murdered on the job."

• • •

"[T-shirts with the slogan 'Destroy All Girls' in very small type on the washing-instructions tag] are awful… I think we've got to take a look at what's going on in the culture as a whole that [anti-female] attitudes get expressed all over the place."
—*political consultant Jacqueline Salit; CNN & Company, May 19, 1997*

"Roseanne started her national television career on the 'Tonight Show' saying, 'Did you hear the one about the woman who stabbed her husband 37 times. I'm really impressed by the restraint that she showed.'… I think that was a big part of her appeal."
—*political consultant Jacqueline Salit; CNN & Company, May 19, 1997*

• • •

On December 30, 2000, the *Washington Post* reported that 115 girl babies and 158 boy babies were killed in the USA in 1997. But what headline did the paper use on that story? "A Matter Of Violent Death and Little Girls." Thirty-seven percent more boys than girls were killed, but the story focused on the girls.

Keep an eye out for this when you go to the movies. When a screenwriter wants the audience to dislike a male character, all the writer has to do is show the character in an argument or disagreement with a female, or show him being unkind to her. There's no need for the audience to know why he's upset with her, and no need to explain his background or the details of the disagreement. The audience will automatically assume that he is wrong; they will be well on the road to not liking him just by virtue of the fact that there is anger or unhappiness between him and a woman.

She's unhappy. He's a bastard. Or a jerk. Let's get him. Case closed. Except for the sentencing, which will now unfold on the screen.

This is feminacentrism at work.

Feminacentrist Spin Control Makes Men Dizzy

"Did you ever notice," a male friend asked me, "that we have the word *misogyny* for anger at women, but we don't have a word—except *misandry*, which no one knows or uses—for anger at men?"

"Yes, I have," I answered. "Isn't that something?"

"It sure is," he said. "It just proves that being angry at men is simply not allowed."

Surprised, I said, "Gosh, I came to an entirely different conclusion."

"How could you possibly come to a different conclusion?" he asked. "It's obvious."

"Well, what's the word," I asked, "for crossing the street against a light or in the middle of a block?"

"That's *jaywalking*," he answered.

"And what's the word for crossing the street at an intersection with a green light?"

"There isn't any word for that. It's just called *crossing the street*."

"And so maybe," I suggested, "the reason we have a word to spotlight anger at women is because we want to punish and discourage it, and the reason we don't have a word for anger at men is because, like crossing the street with a green light, it's perfectly okay."

My friend had no response—other than to insist that surely I must be wrong.

In August 2001, the highly-rated Canadian TV show W-FIVE aired a program on workplace deaths and injuries among youth. The Canadian reality is probably not terribly different from the situation in the States, or anywhere else in the world for that matter. From 1996 thru 2000, according to the Census of Fatal Occupational Injuries, US Bureau of Labor Statistics, 872 young people between the ages of 15 and 19 were killed at work in the USA; 782 were male; 90 were female. W-FIVE never mentioned and never researched a gender component to the problem it was covering, even though all three of the victims it profiled were male.

It is not that the people at W-FIVE are heartless; in fact the producer who faxed me the transcript was a nice as she could be. It's just that we don't think—or perhaps don't want to think—of how the male role is so closely tied to injuries and death.

It is difficult to imagine that a report on anorexia would fail to mention how sex and gender pressures affect girls and women. But it is all too common for us to look male problems squarely in the face and not acknowledge that what's happening to men and boys is happening to them precisely because they are male.

Feminacentrism is the culprit. It demands that we see and pay attention only to problems that affect girls and women. Males are cheap, it says. If they break they can easily be replaced.

In their book *Raising Cain*, psychologists Dan Kindlon and Michael Thompson point out that the Bible story of Cain and Abel is about a man who kills his sibling because he feels his parents love, respect and appreciate his sibling more than they do him.

If females can be thought of as males' siblings, males have a lot of reason to feel like Cain these days. And that's not good for anyone.

Double Standards

Spin Control gives rise to double standards: seeing something as good or acceptable if it involves females and seeing the same thing as bad or intolerable if it involves us. There are probably hundreds or thousands of double standards operating against men and boys.

> "In a classic study in the field of gender research, John and Sandra Cundry videotaped… a nine-month-old infant… They played the ten-minute tape for 204 male and female adults… Some were told the baby was male, others… were told it was female. The adult subjects saw the crying 'girl' baby as frightened, but when they thought they were watching a boy, they described 'him' as angry."
> —*therapist Terrence Real*
> *in his 1997 book* I Don't Want to Talk About It: Overcoming the Secret Legacy of Male Depression

> "Boys are more likely to be scolded and reprimanded in classrooms, even when the observed conduct and behavior of boys and girls does not differ."
> —*Myra and David Sadker, "Report Card #1"*
> *The Mid-Atlantic Center for Sex Equity, American University*

> "Feminine behaviour is the model; it is the standard by which all children's behaviour is judged… During one assembly, the headmistress of this primary school asked the children: 'What does the colour blue make you think of?' A little girl who answered 'flowers' was praised. A boy who enthusiastically answered 'Chelsea' [an English football/soccer team whose color is blue]… was given a pained look and told to think again… Maleness, apparently, is stigmatised everywhere."
> —*Alexander Wade, a teacher in training, in* The Spectator *(UK),*
> *September 2, 2000*

➢ If a woman ends a marriage, she is putting an end to a stifling and oppressive relationship. If a man ends a marriage, he is abandoning his family. If a woman decides not to marry someone, it is her choice for making her life as happy as she can. If a man decides not to marry someone, he is a "womanizer" or "afraid of commitment."

Double Standards of Acceptable Media Behavior

"I personally am livid... Have you considered castration as an option?"
—*NBC co-anchor Katie Couric to a bride who was left standing at the altar*
"The Today Show," November 25, 1997

It is difficult to imagine that a male co-host on national TV would even think of making a similar "joke" about a woman, but it is easy to imagine what would have happened to him if he did, isn't it?

• • •

"I think Hillary [Clinton] is a total babe, and I'd be happy to row her boat, if you know what I mean, just to thank her for all she has done with health care...
"Are you out of your mind, Tony? That's unbelievably crude. You can't say that.
"Why not? Nina Burleigh, a former *Time* magazine White House reporter wrote in *Mirabella*, 'If [President Clinton] had asked me to continue... back in his room... I would have been happy to go there and see what happened.' Later, in an interview with the *Washington Post*, Burleigh declared, 'I'd be happy to give him [oral sex] just to thank him for keeping abortion legal.'"

—*Tony Kornheiser*
Washington Post, *July 12, 1998*

➢ What do you call the story of a spouse who has hot sex with a stranger while the other spouse is dutifully out of town with the kids? Well, that depends. If the cheating spouse is a man, it's another woeful tale of men's selfishness and irresponsibility. If the cheating spouse is a woman, it's *The Bridges of Madison County*, a best-selling "romance," hugely popular among women.

Yes, I'm controlling you, Johnny, but it's only to fill my emotional void.

Why do teachers become sex offenders? If they're female it's because they are "trying to get attention and fill an emotional void." But if they're male it's because they are "interested in the sex and the control."

derived from the Baltimore Sun, *June 10, 2001*

Yes, I stole, and I'm so unselfish I stole for children I don't even have.

In a 1997 Research Study called "Understanding the Sentencing of Women," the British Home Office found that many magistrates distinguished between "troubled" and "troublesome" defendants, and typically applied the first label to women. Some magistrates acknowledged holding the belief that women who stole did so only to feed their children, while men who committed the same crime did so for "selfish" reasons. The study found that some magistrates even applied this sexist double standard to women who had no children and to men who did indeed have children to feed.

derived from an article by John Waters, Irish Times, *April 30, 2001*

Is it because Justice is always portrayed as a woman?

Canterbury University Ph.D. student Samantha Jeffries studied 388 criminal court cases in New Zealand, with 194 males and 194 females committing serious drug, property and violence crimes between 1990 and 1997. She found that even controlling for all other factors such as criminal history, the sex of the defendant had a significant impact on his or her sentence. She found that when the defendant was female the judge searched for an explanation and an excuse to explain away the behavior. Jeffries said she believes that judges still have difficulty believing that women do bad things. "When we're faced with a female who has committed a crime," she said, "it's unbelievable to us. We look for excuses. It goes right back to 'girls are made of sugar and spice and boys of slugs and snails and puppy dog tails'."

derived from the Sunday Star Times, *Auckland, New Zealand*
June 10, 2001

The standard for boy behavior toward girls

"You may never ever hit a girl, no matter what, not even in self-defense and if you ever do we'll thrash you to within an inch of your life to teach you a lesson about violence!"

The standard for girl behavior toward boys

"Did you really slug him? Wow, you go girl!"

In 1995, Disney Studios made "Tom and Huck," a movie based on Mark Twain's beloved novels about Tom Sawyer and Huckleberry Finn. Disney added two scenes that have no basis in the original literature and therefore raise ugly questions about the spirit of our own peculiar era.

Here, Becky Thatcher, with no justification whatsoever, pushes Tom from a bridge into a stream.

And here is Becky slugging Tom after he falls through the ceiling of the church during what was thought to be his funeral. The display of violence by a female against a male was entirely gratuitous, without justification or motivation. Becky certainly suffered no consequences for her behavior.

Disney figured these scenes would be such crowd-pleasers that it put both of them in the movie's preview trailer.

Debunking the Notion of Female Superiority

> "I believe that women are the more spiritually advanced sex."
> —*Erica Jong, Washington Post, December 6, 1992*

➤ If women are so wonderful and kind and loving, why are so many women saying such awful things about their mothers?

> "We [women] have to start looking at our feminine shadow and own that as a part of ourselves and stop projecting it onto males and onto the masculine. It creates the idea that only men abuse. It's only men who are patriarchal. It's only men who are controlling, or greedy, or competitive, all of those negative adjectives that get attached to men and masculinity. Women are capable of just as much viciousness, cruelty and abuse as men."
> —*Carolyn Baker, Ph.D.,*
> *author of* Reclaiming the Dark Feminine

Women are not inherently more peaceful than men.

> "If you talk to the principals, they will tell you that the worst fights to try to break up are those among girls because they tend to be more violent."
> —*Howard Co. (Maryland) School Superintendent Michael E. Hickey; quoted in the* Baltimore Sun, *May 16, 1997*

> "In a 1993 survey of Ontario high school girls, [a] community psychologist… put the following question to them: Defining violence as broadly as they wished, who were they most afraid of? Overwhelmingly, they responded, 'Other girls'."
> —*Patricia Pearson in her 1997 book* When She Was Bad: Violent Women and the Myth of Innocence

➢ Blaming us for war is like blaming women for diaper rash. Both just come with the job.

If you tell a group of people that their primary mission in life is to bring home —and keep —as much bacon as they can, and if there really is no such thing as "enough," conflict among those people is inevitable, especially when bacon is scarce.

➢ When you're at a party or a bar, take a look around. Check it out on TV. Notice how many times women slap, punch or shove men who do or say something the women don't like. It happens so often we don't even see it anymore.

Women do not perpetrate less domestic violence than men do.

> John Archer, professor of psychology at the University of Central Lancashire in Britain and president of the International Society for Research on Aggression, analyzed 99 studies involving 34,000 men and women. He found that women initiate domestic violence more often than men do.
>
> Dr. Malcolm George, a lecturer at London University, researched the claim by women's advocates that women are violent only in response to violence by men. "The view is that women are acting in self-defence but that is not true—50 per cent of those who initiate aggression are women."
>
> *derived from* The Independent *(Britain), November 12, 2000*

> Professor Murray Straus, co-director of the New Hampshire-based Family Research Laboratory, says that the women's activists who propagate bogus and anti-male statistics about domestic violence "are from the 'all men are bastards' branch of feminism." He cited a Stats Canada study involving almost 26,000 Canadians. It found that seven per cent of men and eight per cent of women were assaulted by their partner. "In repeated surveys starting in 1975 [in the U.S].... we get about 10 per cent of men severely assaulting a partner and about 10 per cent of women. It's within one per cent. For both minor and severe assaults the rates are approximately the same."
>
> *derived from* The Calgary Herald *(Canada), November 6, 2000*

> "The research and evidence couldn't be clearer—domestic abuse of men is a problem similar in magnitude to that of abuse of women… And society needs to see that yes, very often it is the 6-foot-2-inch male who is the one getting attacked by his 5-foot-5-inch wife."
>
> —*Carol Ensign, director of Valley Oasis in LA county, one of the few domestic violence shelters in the USA that helps battered men;* Los Angeles Daily News, *August 21, 2001*

> "Female approval of husband assault remains as high now as it was twenty years ago: Twenty-three percent of women believe that 'slapping the cad' is just fine."
> —*Patricia Pearson in her 1997 book* When She Was Bad: Violent Women and the Myth of Innocence

> "Women's violence has become increasingly legitimised. There is a sense now that it's OK to 'slap the bastard.'"
> —*Dr. Anne Campbell, a psychologist at the University of Durham, quoted in* The Independent *(Britain), November 12, 2000*

Women are not naturally more caring, loving and unselfish than we are.

> "Those who have experienced dismissal by the junior high school girls' clique could hardly, with a straight face, claim generosity and nurture as a natural attribute of women."
>
> —*Elizabeth Fox-Genovese
> in her 1991 book* Feminism Without Illusions

> Non-custodial fathers pay 60.0 percent of the child support they are ordered to pay. Non-custodial mothers pay only 46.8 percent.
> *derived from US Census Bureau, Current Population Survey, Table 1, April 1998*

> "When I started researching this book, I was prepared to rediscover the old saw that conventional femininity is nurturing and passive and that masculinity is self-serving, egotistical, and uncaring. But I did not find this. One of my findings here is that manhood ideologies always include a criterion of selfless generosity, even to the point of sacrifice. Again and again we find that 'real' men are those who give more than they take."
>
> —*David Gilmore*
> *in his 1990 book* Manhood in the Making

➤ Why are the two largest male events of recent years—Promise Keepers and the Million Man March—concerned with how men can do an even better job of giving, while the two largest female efforts—NOW and the Million Woman March—are about how women can do an even better job of getting?

> "Feminism: It's all about me... Feminism today is wed to the culture of celebrity and self-obsession."
> —Time *magazine cover story, June 29, 1998*

> At a meeting of 1960s and 1970s feminists in New York, the "veterans" decried the rise of the "me-oriented" culture and the sense of entitlement among many young feminists today. "We have produced a generation of uppity women who feel entitled," feminist author Erica Jong said.
> *derived from Women's eNews, May 26, 2002*

A psychiatrist once told me that in his experience the biggest difference between men and women generally is that women focus on what people need and men focus on what people deserve. At first I didn't get it, but I've since come to see it makes a lot of sense.

Female culture has deep roots in the care of infants. It knows that if you don't give a baby everything it needs it will die. Much of what women need to give babies—breast milk—comes more or less automatically to them. So women most often can say, "yes" (though exhaustion and famine can make it difficult and even impossible).

Male culture has deep roots in providing material goods for women and children. It knows that if you always give a child everything it needs it will always be a child, it will always need and it will never deserve; it will never take care of itself much less help take care of others. Much of what men need to provide can be scarce and hard to come by. So men more often will say "no," and often in saying "no" they are providing an important intangible: a lesson in survival and frugality.

Both points of view are valid and necessary. A band of humans totally dominated by one point of view would quickly die out. If babies got only what they earned, they would die in a few days because they can earn nothing. If babies always got whatever they needed they would never grow to provide for themselves, to say nothing of providing for others. They would always be burdens, never assets, and would drag the tribe quickly to oblivion.

Therefore, women cannot rightly claim that because they say "yes" more they care more.

The tribe needs a flexible, dynamic relationship between male and female values, between focusing on needing and deserving. It's good when a family has that kind of balance between its husband and its wife. It's even better when both the husband and wife have that kind of balance inside themselves, so that the tension and differences between them are not so stark and they are more likely to meet near the middle to begin with.[4]

In fact, the terminology "male values" and "female values" can be misleading if it causes men to think they shouldn't be soft sometimes and women to think they should never be firm. Even though one culture is primarily associated with masculinity and the other is associated primarily with femininity, perhaps we should call the two cultures Culture 1 and Culture A.

> "My 'kind, caring, sharing side' is my 'kind, caring, sharing side' not my 'female side.'"
>
> —*writer Rich Zubaty*

---

[4] The male-female dichotomy mirrors the classic conservative-liberal divide, so balance is important not only in the private raising of children, but in many public policy decisions as well. (How, for instance, can we help poor people without encouraging them to remain poor so that we'll have to continue helping them and they'll continue needing help?) In fact, I think a strong case could be made that the extreme and vitriolic partisanship we've been seeing in Congress of late not only parallels but is actually connected to the extreme distrust and hostility we've developed between male and female cultures in the past thirty years.

Women are not naturally more committed to monogamy than we are.

An old idea that is popular these days is that boys and men are "naturally" interested in having sex with many partners and that girls and women are not (since they're more loving and virtuous and interested in "commitment" only for the pure spiritual value of it). Anthropologist Helen Fisher, in her 1992 book *Anatomy of Love,* says the idea was already well entrenched in people's minds when another anthropologist named Donald Symons came up with an evolutionary explanation for this supposed fact: having sex with lots of women makes it more likely that a man will keep his genes alive into future generations. As Fisher says, "many scholars bought [Symons' explanation] like a better chocolate bar." Now people talk about it at parties as if it were established, even self-evident fact.

But Dr. Fisher points out that women too have their reasons to "cheat" and "play around": to acquire resources from other men, to keep one or more men on backup in case her current man dies or fails her economically, to give her offspring a mix of DNA so they are not all vulnerable to the same diseases, and to seek sexual variety to keep her sex life vibrant.

"[After a female black-capped chickadee hears her mate being outdone by another male in a song contest, she] will sneak out before dawn and meet with [the] rival male for a coupling. Then she flies back home as if nothing happened and continues to live with her partner... The effect of these extra matings is that some chicks in the nest have been fathered by some other male chickadee... And the betrayed male apparently never knows the difference."

—*Associated Press, May 3, 2002*
reporting on a study in the May 3, 2002 issue of the journal Science

[M]ost monkey and ape females are not seeking to mate with the one best male, and to attach themselves to him. Rather they promiscuously solicit matings from multiple males... [so] no one male could ever be certain of paternity. Primate males—including males in our own species—have this problem... [In the old perspective on mothers there is no recognition] that female sexual desire and the peculiarly flexible patterning of sexuality found in many primates evolved so as to manipulate information available to males about paternity... It simply didn't occur to those thinking in terms of "madonna"/"whore" dichotomies that from an evolutionary perspective, the two might be inseparable.

—*anthropologist Sarah Blaffer Hrdy in an interview with her publisher*
about her 2000 book
Mother Nature: A History of Mothers, Infants, and Natural Selection

"In 1999… the American Association of Blood Banks exploded a quiet bomb with a published survey showing that in as many as 28.2 percent of 280,510 genetic samples studied [by DNA analysis], the putative father was not the biological one."
—New Jersey Law Journal, *March 4, 2002*

• • •

"[In cases of questionable or disputed paternity] the overall exclusion rate for 1999 was 28.2% for accredited labs. Exclusion rates for non-accredited US and foreign labs were slightly less at 22.7% and 20.6% respectively." ["Exclusion" refers to the exclusion of the putative father as the biological father.]
—*American Association of Blood Banks Annual Report Summary for 1999 Prepared by the AABB Parentage Testing Standards Program Unit*

Women do not "create life."

➤ The uterus is not a magic vessel. The sperm and egg together are what generate the impulse for new life. Then the embryo takes charge of its own development, using the uterus only for stability and food.

> "The experiment was testimony to the hardy independence of the embryo. One key to the embryo's integrity is its ability to produce a placenta… The fetal placenta is a versatile, opportunistic… organ…. On an endocrine basis, on a hormonal level, the fetus appears to be totally autonomous."
> —Omni Magazine, *December 1985*

➤ An egg without a sperm is like a sperm without an egg. Neither amounts to much.

Asserting Our Own Agenda on Our Own Terms

If, as Einstein said, all things are relative, nothing can be more relative than the relationship between the sexes. Our point of view is as valid as women's, and is much more in need of being heard.

Taking Equal Control of Dating

> Women who use singles telephone chat lines in Australia don't have to pay for the services but men do because the chat line companies got exemptions from anti-discrimination laws by arguing they would go out of business if they had to treat men and women equally. "Women definitely have the upper hand in the dating game," said one company official. "Their reluctance to pay for these type of services is a worldwide phenomenon."
> *derived from the* Herald Sun *(Melbourne), May 21, 2001*

➤ Instead of fretting about whether our dates are the kind of women who want us to open their door, we need to decide whether we're the kind of men who want the kind of women who want us to open their door.

And if you're going to open her door, it might be worth asking what kind of "old-fashioned" things she's going to do for you.

It is in the minds of at least many women to pretty much blithely do what they want to do and be how they want to be, and then expect us to adjust, to figure out how we can service them, how we can win their favor.

> "[The woman] doesn't have to do anything more on the date than show up… don't make it easy for him… he has to do all the work."
>
> —*Ellen Fein & Sherrie Schneider,* The Rules

We need to turn that situation around—at least half-way. We need to be secure in the knowledge that we have something women want and need: maleness, masculinity, a different way of looking and laughing at the world, different ideas of raising kids, penises attached to fully functioning, autonomous human beings. You want me? Okay, I might want you. What do you have in mind?

Ultimately women find male strength to be much more appealing than desperation, malleability and obsequiousness.

➤ Do we have to pay for dates because we make more money, or do we make more money because we have to pay for dates?

———

➤ Women say the rule is "You ask, you pay." Why not "You accept, you pay"?

———

➤ If "you ask, you pay" is really women's rule, does that mean that women who place personal ads pay for the dates they get as a result?

———

➢ How come "you ask, you pay" or "the person who makes more money should pay" isn't the rule when "girlfriends" go out together?

> **And exactly why should we pay for dates?**
>
> "It's just chivalrous… It's nice of you to care about his finances, but remember he is deriving great pleasure from taking you out."
> —*Ellen Fein & Sherrie Schneider,* The Rules
>
> "'The guy should pay [for dates]…' says [ESPN SportsCenter anchor Rich] Eisen…
> "Why is that?… 'Hey, those are the rules,' he says. 'I don't make them. I just follow them.'"
> —Talk Magazine, *September 2000*

A better question

"Any woman who expects the man to pay for everything all the time is behaving like a spoiled princess… A woman who has the means to pay for a date but refuses to do so is saying the pleasure of the man's company is not worth the price of dinner. Why should any man want to waste his time with a woman who has such a low opinion of him?"

—letter to the editor from a woman in Silver Spring, Md.
New York Times, August 31, 2001

Like this woman, for instance

"'Of course the men have to pay and buy you presents. Men have to spoil you. You have to be spoiled,' says [a 26-year-old woman] who works in public relations. 'If you don't think you're a princess you're not going to be treated like one. You have to make sure you know—and they know—you're a princess. This is my feminism. It's the new feminism to say, "I'm expensive. I need lots of attention. I need men to bend over backwards for me."'"

—article by Rebecca Eckler in the National Post (Canada), August 26, 2000

A man quoted by Maureen Dowd in the *New York Times*, August 29, 2001 said. "[Paying for dates] is one of the few remaining ways we can demonstrate our manhood."

Actually, it's one of the many remaining ways we continue to demonstrate our chumphood.

In the same article, a 33-year-old female TV producer in New York told Dowd, "If you offer [to pay] and they accept, then it's over."

One day, when relations between the sexes are more fairly balanced, we'll say "If she doesn't offer by the second date, it's over."

Wouldn't that be powerful?

Aside from who pays, it's also important who asks

Suppose you have a wristwatch and you badly need $200. You might go up to someone and say, "I just paid $400 for this watch last week. Look, here's the receipt. Here's the warranty card. It's legit. I need some cash quick. I'll sell it to you for $200." The other person says, "I don't need a watch. I have a watch. I don't like that watch. I'll give you $100." And you say, "$150." And he says, "$125." And you say, "Deal! I'll take it." And you end up getting $125 for your $400 watch.

Now suppose somebody comes up to you and says, "Man, I need a wristwatch bad! How much did you pay for that one?" And you say, "$400." And he says, "I'll give you $500 for it." And you say, "I don't need the money. I like this watch. It's special. It has sentimental meaning to me." And he says, "I'll give you $600." And you say, "It means so much to me." And he says, "$700." And you say, "Make it $800." And he says "$750." And you say, "$775." And he says, "Deal! I'll take it." And you end up getting $775 for your $400 watch.

What's the difference between the two situations? Why is the watch worth $125 in one transaction and $775 in another? What's the difference?

The difference, as Fred Hayward of Men's Rights, Inc., points out, is that the person who initiates the transaction is almost always in the weaker bargaining position.

Here's the main point about who pays for dates. The more you pay, the more you're setting yourself up to be the one who will provide money in the relationship. The more you are the one responsible for providing money, the fewer options you will have in your future to do anything else.

> "The feminist freeloading doesn't change with marriage. Professional women still want their husbands to get the checks at restaurants, pay the mortgage and get home by 6:30 to help with chores and kids."
> —*Maureen Dowd,* New York Times, *August 29, 2001*

When it comes time to pay for the first date, pick up the tab, smile at your date and say, "This one's on me. And I won't mind a bit if you pick up the next one." Simple. Easy. Fair. And it'll help you find out quickly just what she wants you for.

A Hard Man Is Good to Find

➤ Women enjoy the physical experience of sex at least as much as we do. But, like Tom Sawyer getting the gullible boys to pay him to whitewash his fence, women have us paying them—in one form or another—to do what they want done.

> "Pre-Nineteenth century Western culture assumed that women, not men, were the insatiable sexual aggressors, with men as vulnerable creatures in need of protection."
> —*Historian Peter N. Stearns in his 1990 book*
> Be a Man: Males in Modern Society

➤ Why is sex thought to be something women give and we get?

➢ We need to be more selective about whom we have sex with. A woman should give a man an erection at least three times before he gives it to her once.

> In 1972, a research project called the Boston Couples Study interviewed 462 dating college students. A follow-up study 25 years later found that the men who had not rushed into sex but rather had waited for a committed emotional relationship were more likely to be having happy adulthoods than those who had followed the standard script that says males should have sex as often as they can 'get it.'
> —*author's correspondence with Professor Charles Hill, director of the BCS in 2001*

Equal Options for Men in Jobs and Money

➤ The economy was the very first equal opportunity project. It evolved to help us match the power inherent in women's biological advantage in reproduction.

➤ We earn more money because we focus more on earning money. We need to buy things women don't, like the love and affection of the other sex.

> "Only 14 percent of female middle managers aspire to be CEO; the figure is 45 percent for middle managers who are male."
> —*Newsletter of the Women's Freedom Network*
> *Spring 1997*

➤ Most of us would be happy to say, "Sure, come on, share my money-making. And tell me you'll love me no matter how much money I make, no matter what kind of car I drive."

The price of her love. The love of her life.

"There was a struggle going on inside of me. I mean, he lost his job at the auto body shop when they went [bankrupt] and closed down. Then he couldn't find another one. But it was months and months, and I was trying to live on my welfare check and it just wasn't enough. Finally, I couldn't do it anymore [because] it was just too much pressure on me [even though] he is the love of my life. I told him he had to leave even though I knew it wasn't really his fault… I couldn't take it, so I made him leave."

—*A woman interviewed by researcher Kathryn Edin reported in* The American Prospect, *January 3, 2000*

It's only natural?

Hard economic times in Japan have spurred more and more middle-age wives to cash in their husbands. A divorce consultant in Tokyo said, "Many women believe a husband's job is to be the breadwinner. It is natural for women like that to make the first move in seeking a divorce if they realize that their husbands may not be able to guarantee financial stability and a secure income in the future."

derived from The Daily Yomiuri, *December 6, 2000*

➤ We know that male doctors marry female nurses. How many of us can even imagine a female doctor marrying a male nurse or a talented poet struggling to get by?

> "No matter how strong a woman is, no matter how much of a feminist a woman is, she still tends to look down on men who are not sufficiently aggressive and successful… We still want men to achieve as much or more, and we have contempt for those who don't. They're marginal; they're losers."
> —*writer and professor Jane Young*
> *in* Good Will Toward Men *by Jack Kammer*
>
> "The divorce rate might be lower if women placed more emphasis on men's character and less on their paychecks."
> —*Donna Laframboise, author of* The Princess at the Window

> The 1980 version of the Report of the NOW Project on Equal Education Rights (PEER) talked about how good it would be if "a man could quit a job he hated and take time off to retool, counting on his wife's salary to provide a psychic and financial safety net."
>
> In the 1981 issue of the PEER Report, that male-friendly sentiment was nowhere to be found. Apparently NOW decided that full options were for women only.
>
> This is the first clear fossil evidence I've found of where feminism shifted to pheminism. Women realized that their ability to enjoy many options depended on men enjoying few.
>
> The idea of equal sharing seems to have escaped them, though the rhetoric of equality still echoes loudly through their cant.

➢ They say a woman's work is never done. But if a man is a primary breadwinner, when can he ever say he has won "enough"?

➤ At a party ask your friends, "What's the most valuable thing in this room?" They'll mention expensive things: the stereo, the sofa, the TV. But a much more valuable thing is the air. Remind your friends that at least some of the best things in life are free and there are some priceless things that we might be lacking—despite the fact we earn more money.

There is a difference between something that society values and something that society pays for. Could it be that money is merely artificial valuation for work that is not intrinsically very attractive?

➤ The Number One Reason we earn more money than women do: we have little choice.

Warren Farrell, author of several outstanding books on men and men's issues, was at one time a devoted and loyal supporter of the women's movement and was elected three times to the board of New York City NOW. In *The Liberated Man*, his first book, published in 1976, he urged us to support "women's liberation" on the expectation that as women made their own money they would be less financially dependent on us to support them and we could enjoy some liberation of our own. Sadly, Warren has seen that his prediction has not been borne out. He now observes that as women make more and more money they look more and more upward financially for men they deem worthy. The result has been only more and more economic pressure on us to earn money so women will see us in their rising economic field of vision.

> "[S]leek young women in the Prada-handbag crowd... cast chilly, appraising glances around the room at power-lunch restaurants and dot-com launch parties. You can almost see the thought-balloons over their heads: 'Anyone here making more than me and worth talking to?' Most of [the] female clients [of one professional matchmaker who worked at two dating services in San Francisco for ten years] were over 30. They made a lot of money but were determined to find a man who made even more. Their happiness seemed to depend on it."
> —*columnist Sue Hutchison, San Jose (California) Mercury News*
> *October 1, 2000*

➢ If a man is with his wife when she sees a big, beautiful, expensive house and swoons aloud, "Oooh, I could live like that," the man should spot a woman with a great figure and say, "Oooh, I could make love to her." Call it sensitivity training.

Imagine a women's prison on a hillside. There's a rebellion going on. The inmates are breaking free.

Up the hill is another building—stoic, imperturbable. From inside comes the calm, controlled, orderly chanting of deep, male voices. Nobody's leaving. Must be an Old Boys Club, the women conclude. A real male bastion.

The escapees surge up the hill. "We're going in there and nobody's going to stop us!"

They climb a ledge and peer through a grate. They see men with glazed eyes, straining to turn the heavy wheels of mammoth machines. Now they hear the words of the men's chant. "Man's world. No problems. Man's world. In control."

On the ledge, one of the women snarls, "Look at those jerks! They think they're better than us!"

Another woman asks, "What are they doing?"

A third woman gulps. "That must be how they generate power."

"Oh," the second woman responds as she first notices the transmission lines running down the hill to the pastel prison from which she has escaped. "Good! It's getting dark and I'm cold. I'm going back."

The woman who gulped speaks up, "No! We have to help them get out of there! Don't you see? They'll never do it by themselves!"

"To hell with that," the other women shout back. "Where were they when we needed them?"

➢ Just as it takes money to make money, it takes freedom to make freedom. That's why there has been a women's movement and nothing much to speak of for us. Women were held in minimum security. But men are at hard labor. Society needs to keep us under tight control so we don't get away from our "important work."

> "Nothing against work, money and power, but a 'man's world' just isn't all it's cracked up to be… [T]here's a reason it's called 'work.' Women aren't the only ones who don't make it to the top; most men don't either… I'll teach my daughter she can be anything she wants: the president of the United States, or the class mother, or maybe someday, both. Should my son have fewer choices?"
> —*Susan Estrich, USA Today, March 14, 1996*

➢ Maybe it's true that in a race from New York to Los Angeles we get a headstart by being in Cleveland. But what if where we really want to go is Paris or London or Istanbul?

At what point does an advantage become an obligation?

In a car, the engine would be considered "more important" than the stereo. But where would you rather be, under the hood where it's hot, greasy, noisy and dangerous or in the passenger compartment where it's cool, comfortable and safe?

Which would be granted its choice, a stereo that wanted to ride along under the hood for a while or an engine that wanted to sit in the back seat and take it easy for a spell?

Being "more important" can be the exact opposite of a privilege.

Some supposedly intelligent women apparently believe that only women have to make "tremendous personal sacrifice" in order to succeed.

"Women lawyers who have succeeded often have done so at tremendous personal sacrifice. Many attribute their achievements to a willingness and ability to adapt to a work culture that is defined by and for white men. Many placed family or personal life at risk as they emulated the male model of 'commitment' to the law… By refusing to play a role created by and for men, women will ascend the mountain free of constraints."

*—"Unfinished Business"
American Bar Association Report
on Women in the Legal Profession*

Do the womenfirsters who wrote this report actually suppose that men are "free of constraints"?

What makes the "male model" male other than men's willingness to submit to it?

➤ Saying that we shape business and industry to suit our needs is like saying that water makes the bucket round.

To give ourselves purpose and value, we took on the difficult mission of economic production and we adapted ourselves to accomplish it.

An especially ludicrous example of the idea that we shape the world to suit ourselves was in *Time* magazine's Special Issue on Women in the Fall of 1990, which said that prison is "a system designed and run by men for men."

> In his 1997 book *I Don't Want To Talk About It*, Terrence Real says that his father, who grew up poor, worked his way through art school with the help of the GI Bill. When two children were born the man added two paying jobs to his school workload and got little sleep for three years. Yet he made the dean's list and his art work was widely praised and admired. But since he had a wife and two kids depending on him for income he switched his major from fine art to industrial design. "Years later," writes Real, "he told me that a part of him had died on the day he went to the registrar's office to make the change."
>
> That was years ago. Have things changed? In *Reason* magazine, June 2001, writer Cathy Young observed, "In one couple I know, the father had to drop out of a graduate program in music when he learned that a baby was on the way; he finds his current corporate job boring and exhausting and hates the long hours away from his son. The mother, who quit an office job she never much liked, seems to be enjoying her time at home. Who's making the sacrifice?"

> "I've sacrificed a lot of stuff for my family because I had to go to work. I missed a lot of stuff in my life. And this is what we get out of it right here. It really hurts. It really does hurt bad."
> —*A 55-year-old man who was on strike against a paper mill where he had worked for 25 years; NPR "All Things Considered," August 21, 2001*

➤ Options are commodities that come with a price whether they are exercised or not. Women can't demand more options and also demand equal pay.

Oh, but they can if they want to. And they do.

"In the 1960s, when women first muscled into the work force, at-home moms all but apologized for what they did. But once those same boomer women started families (often late in their 30s), staying home with the kids became the preferred thing to do… 'A lot of women my age don't feel a big need to work because they know they can if they want to,' says… a [32-year-old] mother of two… [Barnard College economics professor Diane] Macunovich says… '[W]omen are using their earnings to buy back personal time.'… A higher portion of women are choosing 'women's work,' such as nursing and teaching. It's no coincidence that these jobs offer many options for part-timers."

—*Jane Bryant Quinn, Newsweek, July 17, 2000*

And it's no coincidence "women's work" pays less.

> **"As women"? Didn't they say they
> wanted to come to work "as equals"?**
>
> "Why should commitment [to work] be demonstrated by working 100 hours per week? As women, we have other options to explore…"
>
> —Laura Bellows
> chair of the American Bar Association
> Commission on Women in the (Legal) Profession;
> Ms. Magazine, November 1995

> "The most important reasons for the 'gender gap' have little to do with employer bias. Increasingly, the gap is the result of choices women make as they seek to maximize their own happiness and achieve a broad mix of life goals."
>
> —Katherine Kersten
> Newsletter of the Women's Freedom Network, Spring 1996

> "Economist Nancy Pfotenhauer ... said women often choose to take jobs that pay less for flexibility and time for children and family...
> 'Women make decisions all the time based on things other than salary—enjoyment of the job and ability to have time with their families,' she said."
> —*Associated Press, April 3, 2001*

> "Single women who have never married, live alone and have full-time jobs earn more than their male equivalents by 28 cents per hour... [S]ingle women earn 101.6 percent of single men's hourly earnings across the full spectrum of occupations, education levels and age."
> —*press release from the Employment Policy Foundation; April 2, 2002*

➤ Here's a deal: we'll make sure that women are equally represented in corporate boardrooms when they make sure we are equally represented among employees who take family leave.

The Men's Bureau

The Women's Bureau of the US Department of Labor has a budget of $8.4 million and 72 full-time personnel in its DC headquarters and ten regional offices around the country. Its mission is "to formulate standards and policies which shall promote the welfare of wage-earning women, improve their working conditions, increase their efficiency, and advance their opportunities for profitable employment."

It is time now for a parallel body for men. The Men's Bureau's mission would be "to formulate standards and policies which shall promote the welfare of wage-earning men, improve the flexibility of their working hours, enable their equal involvement in parenting, and advance their opportunities for rewarding parenthood and a healthy family life."

How is that a concern of the Labor Department? For one thing, unless we're going to impose artificial quotas, women's equality in the workplace depends on our equality outside it. And the Men's Bureau could help workers be balanced and healthy. Harmonious family life is the most effective and least expensive Employee Assistance Program of all.

Equal Options for Men in Marriage and Parenting

> **Afraid? Yes, but not of commitment.**
>
> The median age of first marriage for men in the US has climbed to 27, the oldest it has ever been. Researchers who surveyed a pilot sample of 60 bachelors between the ages of 25 and 33 found that young men are often leery of marriage because they worry about marrying the wrong person, about having to make unreasonable compromises, about the pressures of being a husband and about huge financial loss if the marriage ends in divorce. A common remark from the men was that a woman in divorce will "take you for all you've got." The researchers urged further study.
>
> *derived from the* Washington Times, *June 26, 2002*

➤ It is statistically true that married men are more successful than unmarried men. But are they more successful because they're married or are they married because they're more successful?

➤ Men's slang expression for marriage—being "hitched"—did not arise from nowhere.

➤ If marriage is as much for fathers as it is for mothers, why is it called <u>Matri</u>mony?

➤ The same folly that tells us a woman's place is in the home tells us our place is anywhere but in the home; the tragedy for us is that home is where the heart is.

➤ We are fathers, not babysitters.

> **Shouldn't She Know Better?**
> "I want to thank my husband who is home babysitting."
> —*Congresswoman Susan Molinari*
> *May 28, 1997*
> *on announcing her resignation from Congress*
> *to take a job with CBS*

➤ We kept women out of the male domain by using laws and rules to bar them. But those kinds of barriers are obvious and easy to tear down. Women keep us out of the female domain—where our children are—just by festooning it with lace and pink ribbons. And women can say, "Come in if you want; we're not stopping you."

And when we go in, we can ignore the pink lace and frilly stuff, and develop our own style of parenting, just as women abandoned the severe, mannish suit for their careers in industry and asserted a female style of doing business.

> "We don't talk about it very much, but there are a lot of power and control issues in any relationship. I think that some women want control of the kitchen and nursery, and they do, on an unconscious level, shoo men away. What I hear that keeps men from being involved is that women impose their personal standards. Men tell me, 'I dress the child and she says, "Oh, she's too hot," or I dress the child and, "Oh, he's too cold."' The natural reaction of any human being is to say, 'Well, if I don't do it to your satisfaction, then you do it!'… I think it's necessary [for women] to keep their lips buttoned sometimes and not impose their particular standards… Men and women have different styles; both are good, and kids need both."
>
> —*Gayle Kimball, Ph.D., author of* The 50-50 Marriage
> *in* Good Will Toward Men *by Jack Kammer*

> "I know in my case, we really don't mean it when we say we want an equal partner," [Suzanne Braun Levine, a founding editor of *Ms.* magazine and former editor of the *Columbia Journalism Review*] said. "We want a competent executive assistant... We subtly discourage our husbands from learning by doing it. We throw up our hands and say, 'Let me do it.' That's very demoralizing."
> —*quoted by Judy Mann,* Washington Post, *September 1, 2000*
>
> • • •
>
> "Women… may complain that men don't do enough with their children but the truth is that mothers often don't allow fathers to have much input. They'll see a father fumbling as he tries to make the formula for the baby's bottle. Instead of letting him get on with it, they get bossy and possessive, and say: 'Give the bottle to me; I can do it quicker myself.'"
> —*best-selling British author Shirley Conran*
> Sunday Times *(London), October 1, 2000*

➢ Just as some men were upset by the idea that women could be competent doctors and astronauts, some women don't like the fact that we can be perfectly adequate, independent parents.

> **A Little Test to Give to Women**
>
> "Imagine that you are home on a Saturday afternoon, sitting quietly in your living room with your favorite magazine, content to hear your child happily riding her tricycle outside. Then you hear the child take a tumble. She is not seriously hurt, but her cries grow louder as she runs into the house for comfort for her injured knee. Your heart goes out to her as she comes racing toward you. You close your magazine and put it aside to make room for her on your lap. With arms outstretched, she runs right past you crying, 'Daddy!'
>
> How does that make you feel?"

> "It is easier for men to take on the nurturing of children than for women to give up some of it. The greatest emotional challenge for women is to allow men to nurture children in their own manner."
> —*Joan Peters, author*
> When Mothers Work, *1997*

➤ Men said that women don't belong in industry because they lack the "business instinct." Now women are saying that we don't belong with children because we lack the "nurturing instinct."

Isn't he beautiful?

When their babies are born, new fathers often experience "engrossment," much like the feelings that women experience immediately after birth:

Fathers prefer to look at their own baby and perceive the newborn as attractive and beautiful.

Fathers like to touch, pick up, move, hold, and play with the baby.

Fathers remember the unique features and characteristics of their baby and feel they can distinguish their own baby from others.

Fathers perceive their baby as perfect even if it has unsightly imperfections.

Fathers feel extreme elation over their new baby.

Fathers feel an increased sense of self-esteem because of the new baby.

derived from "A Perspective on Father-Infant Interactions" by Oliver H. McKagen, Radford University

Natural Fathers

The male Emperor Penguin stands straight up for hours upon hours with his and his mate's fertilized egg safely perched between his feet and huge rolls of his belly's warm fat to protect his incubating baby from freezing 100 mph Antarctic winds.

The male African Sand Grouse ranges far and wide—sometimes as far as 50 miles—to find water for his kids. He soaks himself in the water, heads home and lets the kids suck the water from the feathers on his breast.

The male Sea Horse has a pouch in which he carries his and his mate's fertilized eggs. The eggs attach to his body and get their food through his blood vessels. In about two weeks, when the babies are ready to come out of his pouch, he gives birth.

The male Giant Water Bug protects his eggs from fish by carrying them on his back until they hatch.

The male Egyptian Mouth Breeder is a fish who hatches eggs in his mouth. After his babies are born they'll swim right back into his mouth when they're scared.

derived from an unpublished manuscript by writer Kay Haugaard and from the Washington Post, *June 15, 2001*

Fathers should be more involved!
(But not more than mothers want.)

- Only about one mother in four thinks that fathers should play a fifty-fifty role in raising the children.
- Mothers want fathers to help more with children, but not to overshadow their role as primary parent.
- Two out of three mothers seem threatened by a father's equal participation in child rearing.
- Mothers themselves may be subtly putting a damper on men's involvement with their children because they are so possessive of their role as primary nurturer.

derived from The Motherhood Report
Louis Genevie, Ph.D. and Eva Margolies, 1987

"The research seems to show that mothers can be real gatekeepers... that the level of contact a father has with the kids has more to do with the mother's characteristics than with the father's."

—*Richard Weissbourd, instructor on childhood issues at Harvard's Kennedy School of Government;* Los Angeles Times, *March 1, 1995*

> "The early women's movement could have been explained in simple terms as 'women can do what men can do.' Now we need to proceed to the next step by realizing men can do what women can do."
>
> —*Gloria Steinem*
> *on NPR "Weekend Edition," February 9, 1992*

> "When you have to work late and need someone to look after your kids until you can get home, where do you turn? You call another mother and she bails you out. When that mother discovers she needs to be out of town on the day it's her turn to drive the preschool carpool, does she ask her husband to fill in? No. She calls you, and you gladly switch with her."
>
> —*"The Motherhood: An Unbreakable Union"*
> *by Olivette Orme*
> The Wall Street Journal, *May 9, 1997*

Who gets to stay with the kids?

Phil Donahue was on the TV in the waiting room of an auto shop where I was getting an oil change. The topic was "Men who stay home with their kids." When the mechanic came to tell me my car was ready, he stopped to watch the show. "What do you think of that?" I asked, fully expecting him to say something about child rearing not being "real man's work." "I'd love to do that," he answered, "but my wife took that job. She didn't even ask. She just took it."

> "No developing society that needs men to leave home and do 'their thing' for the society ever allows young men in to handle or touch their newborns. There's always a taboo against it. For they know that, if they did, the new fathers would become so hooked that they would never get out and do 'their thing' properly."
> —*Margaret Mead*
> *quoted in* Maternal-Infant Bonding *by Klaus and Kennell*
> *Moseby Press, St. Louis 1976*

> Among 18-to-24-years-olds, 48% of men and 66% of women said that if they had the opportunity, they might be interested in staying at home and raising children.
> *derived from Time magazine's Fall 1990 Special Issue on Women*
>
> Among 18-to-24-year-olds, 21% of men and 31% of women said they would choose to stay home full-time and care for their families if they could.
> *derived from the Whirlpool Foundation Study by the Families and Work Institute, May 1995*
>
> **Imagine how we would answer if there was more social support and acceptance for fathers staying home.**

➢ Ask high school girls what combinations and sequences of work and parenting they can realistically imagine for themselves. Then put the same question to the boys. And then ask yourself how far we have come in our efforts to achieve equal opportunity between the sexes.

➢ Women staying home with the kids is not just about breastfeeding. Children don't normally nurse beyond the age of two and, besides, the pattern is the same for women, including adoptive mothers, who don't breastfeed at all.

➢ If women can pump their breasts to leave milk at daycare centers with strangers is there any reason they couldn't do it to leave milk at home with fathers?

> "[T]oday's working stiff really enjoys no more meaningful options than did his father, the pathetic guy in the gray flannel suit who was pilloried as a professional hamster and an emotional cripple."
>
> —*Kyle Pruett, M.D.*
> *a psychiatrist at the Yale Child Studies Center*
> *author of* The Nurturing Father
> *quoted in* Time *magazine's Fall 1990 Special Issue on Women*

> "Traditional work patterns lock women into second rate careers and lock men out of family life, risking damage to the mental health of both sexes. There's even more prejudice against men than there is against women if they attempt to build careers around family responsibilities."
>
> —*Dr. Carolyn Quadrio*
> *psychiatrist and author of a study on part-time work, 1996*
> *Australian Associated Press, April 17, 1996*

➢ Which would you rather have: a heartfelt Fathers Day card every year, or a slim chance of being in the history books after you're dead?

➢ Sure women's work is devalued. It's devalued by women to make it unattractive to men. It's devalued by men because, in sour grapes fashion, we try to convince ourselves that we don't want it.

> **Interview with a Womenfirster:
> Phyllis Schlafly**
>
> Jack Kammer: What if I was the kind of man, like a lot of men who have confided to me, who is sick to death of the corporate world and in a heartbeat would stay home to take care of their kids because they love them so much and they know the business world is a crock?
>
> Phyllis Schlafly:… That's their problem. As I look around the world about me, I just don't find there are many [women] who really want the so-called non-traditional relationships.
> —*a radio interview, WCVT-FM (now WTMD)*
> *Towson University, Maryland*
> *January 5, 1989*

Does every man want to stay home with his kids, even part-time, even temporarily? Certainly not. But every man should have as much opportunity to include those options in his life as women do, just as women demand the right to pursue business careers equally with men.

> "There isn't any job that's going to bring the fulfillment that marriage and children and family bring… They offer many rewards… Careers are no substitute for children and grandchildren… In America it's wonderful to be a woman."
> —*Phyllis Schlafly, speaking at a women's college in Virginia October 14, 1997*

Treatment of Fathers in Divorce

Respect for fatherhood is good for all men whether they have kids or not, just as equal employment opportunity is good for all women, whether they are looking for a job or not. Disrespect for fatherhood is based on bad stereotypes about all of us. Those stereotypes affect you adversely in every relationship you have.

➢ If raising kids is so menial and degrading, why do women fight us so bitterly in divorce for the opportunity to do it?

> *It's not menial and degrading, of course. But by describing it that way women hope to make it unattractive to us so they can keep it for themselves. "What big strong man like you would want to change diapers and burp babies all day?"*

➢ Don't be fooled by the claim that we win half of all custody battles. Most of the men who invest tens of thousands of dollars in full fights for custody are the ones with extraordinarily solid cases. So even if the claim were true it would still mean that of the very most winnable cases, half still lose.

> "The high success rate of men in custody battles is another contender for the Phony Statistics Hall of Fame."
> —*Cathy Young in her 1999 book* Ceasefire!: Why Women and Men Must Join Forces to Achieve True Equality

➤ It is widely reported that men's standard of living goes up after divorce. But did any financial advisor ever tell you to get married, raise kids and then have your wife divorce you so your standard of living would go up?

Let's focus on the Standard of Loving, a measure of the affection, caring and closeness that one feels with one's children; it clearly plummets for most fathers after divorce.

➤ If someone kidnaps your children, and you save a few dollars each month on food and clothing, do you feel that your standard of living has risen?[†]

➤ For a man to be considered half as good a parent as a woman, he has to be two times better.

[†] Thanks to Fred Hayward, director of MR, Inc.

- Some people say we seek custody only as a way of bargaining for lower child support payments. An equally sexist comment would be that women seek custody only to live in the household the father will provide for the children.

- The rebuttable presumption of innocence in crime cases ("innocent until proven guilty") is not "forced acquittal." Similarly, a rebuttable presumption for joint custody is not "forced joint custody," as its detractors try to label it. A father should be presumed a valuable parent unless someone can prove otherwise.

- If joint custody is a bad idea, then we need Affirmative Action in custody decisions to remedy entrenched biases against fathers.

- Would we expect a mother without custody to continue to cook and clean for her ex-husband? Then why do we expect a noncustodial father to keep providing money, especially to an ex-wife who interferes with his "visitation" time? Why do we enforce child support, but not "visitation" rights?

➢ It is admirable that a man facing divorce is reluctant typically to say anything to sully the reputation of, as he might put it, "the mother of my children." Why is a woman unlikely to evidence similar concern or even to use the phrase "the father of my children"?

Consider this as a definition of "family": A group of people guided by one or more adults whose purpose is to ensure harmony between the sexes for future generations by honoring fatherhood as well as motherhood, manhood as well as womanhood, masculinity as well as femininity; not necessarily the same thing as "a woman with children."

> Children who grow up with single mothers are nine times more likely to develop bad opinions of the non-custodial parent than are children who grow up with single fathers.
> *derived from a speech by Warren Farrell, Ph.D., author of* Father and Child Reunion, *on the National Mall in Washington, Fathers Day 2002*

➢ If society wants fathers to be more invested in their kids, fathers need to know their investment is protected.

Equal Parenting Opportunity Commission

The US Equal Employment Opportunity Commission works "to ensure equality of opportunity by vigorously enforcing federal legislation prohibiting discrimination in employment. It uses investigation, conciliation, litigation, coordination, regulation in the federal sector, and education, policy research, and provision of technical assistance to achieve this end."

We need a commission whose mission statement substitutes "parenting" for "employment." Isn't equal parenting at least as important to a healthy nation as equal employment?

Isn't bias against men as fathers at least as harmful as bias against women as employees?

> "If the mother tells you one thing [about how much child support she's getting] and the father tells you something else, then the father is a God damned liar."
> —*a nationally respected demographer moderating a child support discussion panel at a conference in 1988, quoted by Sanford Braver, Ph.D.*
> *in his 1998 book* Divorced Dads: Shattering the Myths

Does anyone feel a chill?

In July 1986, I met with Anne Rosewater, Deputy Staff Director of the US House of Representatives Select Committee on Children, Youth and Families in Washington. I said that men often feel frozen out of government action on family issues.

Ms. Rosewater said nothing could be further from the truth. "Here," she said. "Take our mailing list form. Tell your people we want to know what's on their minds."

It was only when I got home that I noticed the problem.

"Listed below," the form said, "are the categories which now comprise our mailing list. Please check the three you have the greatest interest in, and return to us. We will do our best to keep you informed of the Committee's work in these areas."

The form included twenty-two categories in alphabetical order. Women's Issues was one. I looked at the middle of the list. Literacy, Mental Health, Military Families.

Men's Issues? Nowhere to be found. Fathers' Issues? Ditto.

I wrote to Ms. Rosewater. She ignored my first letter, but after I sent another she wrote that she was "reluctant" to add men's concerns to the form. "It is not possible for every group or individual to be represented on the list," she said, as if fatherhood was a marginal, narrow, special interest in the eyes of the Special Joint Committee on Children, Youth and Families.

Finally, I wrote to the congressman who chaired the Committee.

> In April 1987, I received a new mailing list form with no cover letter, explanation, apology, gratitude or invitation to make further contact. The form listed Men's Issues—tacked on at the end, out of alphabetical order, and below Women's Issues.
>
> I filled out the form and checked "Men's Issues," but never received a single piece of information from the committee before it ceased operation years later.

There is much more to be said about the unfairness visited upon fathers in divorce. Two of the best sources are:

- *Father and Child Reunion: How to Bring the Dads We Need to the Children We Love* by Warren Farrell, Ph.D. (January 2001)
- *Divorced Dads: Shattering the Myths* by Sanford Braver, Ph.D. and Diane O'Connell (October 1998)

Domestic Violence Bigotry: the Maternalist Backlash

There is a lot of joy in helping kids grow up happy and strong. It's one of the very best kinds of gold a person can have in his life. Right now that gold is owned and controlled by women. And as hard as we resisted women getting equality in the monetary marketplace we're seeing women fight even more fiercely to keep us subordinate and second-class in the arena of parental love and joy. Their gold, after all, is much more beautiful and powerful than ours ever was. And they know it.

➤ Just as men tried to keep women out of jobs by playing on sexist stereotypes of women as ditzes and bimbos, women are trying to keep us out of parenting by playing on sexist stereotypes of us as batterers and abusers.

> "Elaine Epstein, former president of the Massachusetts Women's Bar Association… [wrote a newsletter article about] 'the frenzy surrounding domestic violence… The facts have become irrelevant,' she wrote… 'Everyone knows that restraining orders and orders to vacate are granted to virtually all who apply, lest anyone be blamed for an unfortunate result… In many [divorce] cases, allegations of abuse are now used for tactical advantage.'"
>
> —*Cathy Young, writing in* Salon, *October 25, 1999*

Why do pheminists propagate their domestic violence lie? For the same reason racists propagate the Depraved Negro stereotype. To keep us "in our place." For pheminists, our place is away from "their" children. The more we express our desire to be full and equal parents to our children, the more pheminists feel the need to tell their lies, to suggest none too subtly that we are not to be trusted with gentle little children.

The irony is that intelligent people see racists for what they are. Pheminists, on the other hand, are still thought to be progressive.

> For *Women of the Klan* by Kathleen M. Blee [University of California Press, paperback edition 1992], the publisher's description says, "Ignorant. Brutal. Male. One of these stereotypes of the Ku Klux Klan offers a misleading picture. In *Women of the Klan*, sociologist Kathleen Blee unveils an accurate portrait of a racist movement that appealed to ordinary people throughout the country. In so doing, she dismantles the popular notion that politically involved women are always inspired by pacifism, equality, and justice."
>
> In her review of this book in the *Los Angeles Times* (September 1, 1991), Barbara Ehrenreich wrote, "I must now live with the fact that the Klan contained 'all the better people'… even Quakers, political reformers and (this is the truly discomforting part) *feminists*… *Women of the Klan* stands before us as carefully garnered, irrefutable evidence that women are capable of asserting their gender rights in the most noisome settings."

ACTION ALERT ON "FATHERS' RIGHTS" (The Backlash Manifesto)
National Organization for Women, 1996

WHEREAS organizations advocating "fathers' rights," whose members consist of non-custodial parents, their attorneys and their allies, are a growing force in our country; and

WHEREAS the objectives of these groups are to increase restrictions and limits on custodial parents' rights and to decrease child support obligations of non-custodial parents by using the abuse of power in order to control in the same fashion as do batterers; and

WHEREAS these groups are fulfilling their objectives by forming political alliances with conservative Republican legislators and others and by working for the adoption of legislation such as pre-sumption of joint custody, penalties for "false reporting" of domes-tic and child abuse and mediation instead of court hearings; and

WHEREAS the success of these groups will be harmful to all women but especially harmful to battered and abused women and children; and

WHEREAS efforts of well-financed "fathers' rights" groups are expanding, sharing research and tactics state by state; and

WHEREAS many judges and attorneys are still biased against women and fathers are awarded custody 70% of the time when they seek it per the Association of Child Support Enforcement;

THEREFORE BE IT RESOLVED that the National Organization for Women (NOW) begin a national alert to inform members about these "fathers' rights" groups and their objectives through articles in the National Now Times (NNT); and

BE IT FURTHER RESOLVED that, as a part of this alert, NOW establish a clearinghouse for related information by sharing with NOW state and local Chapters the available means to challenge such groups, including the current research on custody and support, sample legislation, expert witnesses, and work done by NOW and other groups in states where "fathers' rights" groups have been active;

BE IT FURTHER RESOLVED, that NOW encourage state and local Chapters to conduct and coordinate divorce/custody court watch projects to facilitate removal of biased judges; and

BE IT FINALLY RESOLVED, that NOW report to the 1997 National Conference on the status and result of this national alert whereupon its continuation or expansion will be considered.

This Action Alert reveals paranoia among women terrified by the thought of men sharing equally in parenting. If judges are so biased against women, why would NOW want to keep divorces in court rather than shift them to mediation?

There was a time when feminists insisted on gender-neutral language about parenting. They said quite rightly that always being depicted as the primary caretakers of children made it difficult for them to be seen as anything else. But now, according to the *Ottawa Citizen*, June 7, 2001, women's groups in Canada are outraged that official documents describing a conference on divorce and family issues are gender-neutral. "This is an astounding omission given that women have overwhelmingly been, and continue to be, the primary caregivers of children," said one of the leaders. Predictably, she then raised the specter of "male violence" to reinforce the wall around women's domain. "Women's organizations believe the outcome of this consultation will jeopardize the rights and safety of women and children," she said.

In an article published in the *National Post* on June 14, 2001, heroic Canadian journalist Donna Laframboise analyzed the 56-page document these women issued. She found that the word "father" appears 54 times, but not once in a favorable context. Twenty-four times the word is neutral; the other thirty times refer to abusive fathers, sex-offender fathers, fathers who want to "control the mother," fathers who abandon or kidnap their children, and fathers who want to spend more time with their children only so they will then have to pay less child support. Some form of the word "abusive" appears 155 times, "violent" or "violence" appear 183 times, "assault" or "assaulted" are used 26 times. The authors refer to men's alleged desire to dominate and control women and children 24 times.

At its most fundamental, the men's movement is a civil rights struggle. It won't be easy.

"Herjury":
False Allegations of Sexual Misconduct

We are easy targets of herjury. We are always suspects if not presumed guilty in matters of sexual impropriety.

So dangerous is male sexuality, in fact, that in March 2001 British Airways told a traveling executive that he would have to change seats because two unaccompanied children were sitting next to him on the plane. We can imagine the conversation between the man and the flight attendant who wanted him to move:

> *Okay, so there are two unaccompanied children sitting next to me. And?*
> *And they're children.*
> *And?*
> *And they're unaccompanied.*
> *And?*
> *And... you know.*
> *No, I don't know. And what?*
> *And you're male!*
> *And?*

*And they're sitting next to you.
And?
And, you know, you're male and all and they're unaccompanied and they're sitting there right next to you and you might, you know…
Might what?
You might molest them!*

The flight attendant said it was "company policy."

It's a good thing the executive "got uppity" and demanded and won an apology from the airline. He won a victory for us all.

➤ We'd be more enthusiastic about stamping out sexual harassment if women were more enthusiastic about stamping out false allegations of sexual harassment.

> "Her testimony was an insult because she lied. She knew what the game was… and she played it to her advantage, but when she didn't like the way it was being played, she cried 'foul ball'."
> —*the forewoman of a jury in Milwaukee, talking about a woman who alleged sexual harassment at work;* Washington Post, *October 5, 1997*

> "Male judges are mostly paternalistic, and don't feel so strongly about a boss who fails to promote a woman, but they feel very strongly indeed about a woman who is sexually mistreated on the job. So I always advise my clients in employment discrimination cases that if the facts can support the allegation <u>in any way</u> they should also file a charge of sexual harassment."
> —*A lawyer conducting a workshop at the 1987 NOW convention (emphasis was hers)*

> **A Feminacentrist Discussion of False Allegations of Sexual Harassment**
>
> David Brinkley: "Sam, are you saying that any woman has the power now, will under these new laws we're talking about, the power to destroy a man by making charges that he cannot disprove?"
>
> Sam Donaldson: "I don't think a woman any more than a man would do that, though, simply willy-nilly. I mean it takes some sort of a sick mind to want to do that."
>
> Brinkley to Barbara Walters: "What do you think about that?"
>
> Walters: "I don't think that that will happen. I think that it will make men perhaps more conscious, this is what we have seen this week, more conscious of how women feel, not just in terms of sexual harassment, but in sexual discrimination, which has not come up here…"
>
> —*"This Week with David Brinkley," ABC News
during the Clarence Thomas-Anita Hill hearings, October 13, 1991*

➢ A false allegation of rape can have consequences as severe as—or even worse than—an actual rape. Why is it punished so lightly, if at all?

> "In [1990 and 1991] women in [seven Washington, DC-area jurisdictions] filed 1,842 rape reports, and police concluded that 439 were unfounded....
>
> "[One] woman said she lied because she needed an excuse for having been late to work."
>
> —*Washington Post, June 27, 1992*

Ah, Chivalry...

> "Our philosophy is that a woman who would file a false rape report needs counseling, not jail time."
> —*Lt. Dan Davis, Howard County (Maryland) Police Department*
> Washington Post, *June 27, 1992*

> "People can be charged with virtually no evidence... If a female comes in and says she was sexually assaulted, then on her word alone, with nothing else—and I mean nothing else, no investigation—the police will go right out and arrest someone... Too many prosecutors just take the word of the female—that's it—and don't investigate. I think if they did investigate, they would find false accusations... [Prosecutors] have visions, I suppose, of women's groups going to the press, of being personally attacked by women's groups... It's all a public relations issue; they're just terrified of being raked over the coals."
> —*Rikki Klieman, criminal defense attorney and former prosecutor* in Good Will Toward Men *by Jack Kammer*

➤ Women coined the emotionally powerful phrase "date rape" to identify a danger they face. We need to popularize "fake rape" to call attention to a problem that threatens us.

The criteria for concluding a rape allegation is false can be debated but false allegations of rape are not rare. A study by Eugene J. Kanin, Ph.D. of Purdue University found 41 per cent to be false; two samples analyzed by Charles P. McDowell, Ph.D. of the US Air Force Office of Special Investigations found 27 per cent and 60 per cent false. Pheminists, however, insist the figure is two per cent ("no more than in other crimes") referring to "FBI statistics" that just don't exist.

➤ Most newspapers will not publish the names of alleged victims of sex crimes, but will publish the names of the accused. But if the accused denies the charges, isn't he claiming to be the victim of a sex crime, namely a false accusation of rape?

> "The names of suspects in rape cases should be protected like those who lodge such complaints, the attorney for Dallas Cowboys star Michael Irvin said Sunday. The remarks came two days after police cleared his client, saying that a woman's rape allegations involving Irvin and teammate Erik Williams were unfounded… A police spokesman said that the department is comfortable with how it handled the case, including releasing the suspects' names on the police report—a decades-old policy."
> —*Associated Press, January 12, 1997*

> "A former topless dancer pleaded guilty yesterday to perjury, admitting she alone decided to falsely accuse two Dallas Cowboys players of sexual assault."
> —USA Today, *September 16, 1997*

Abuse Abuse: "That devil made me do it."

Abuse Abuse is a variation on Herjury's theme.

Houston housewife Andrea Yates drowned her five kids in a bathtub in 2001. Womenfirsters insist it was her husband's fault for being "abusive."

Forest technician Terry Barton started a fire that brought at least six people to their deaths and destroyed more than a hundred homes in Colorado in 2002. Womenfirsters say it was her husband's fault for sending her the "abusive" letter (she claims) she was burning when (she claims) the fire got out of control. (She tried blaming a particular male camper first, and even provided his minivan's license number, but investigators were able to expose that lie and save him from her shameless frame job.)

When women murder their husbands, Womenfirsters reflexively rush to their defense, often claiming the husbands were—you guessed it—"abusive." The premier "expert" on the dubious Battered Women's Syndrome, which seeks to exonerate murderous women who (claim they) were abused, is Lenore Walker, one of the "experts" whose shoddy work on the Super Bowl domestic violence hoax we talked about on page 38. (That ought to give you confidence that you're safe in your own home and your wife or girlfriend couldn't kill you with impunity if she wanted to.)

When a man and woman commit a crime together, prosecutors invariably assume the man is the truly guilty party while the woman was only a hapless—maybe she was abused!—dupe in the male's nefarious plot. They'll make a deal with her and she'll cry on the witness stand and explain to the jury how the bad, bad man was bad, bad, bad. And she was afraid. And she was abused. (And she was a perfect angel to him and to society at large.) He stews, maybe fries; she walks.

So, in large measure, we live in a society in which women can reckon they have a fair shot at getting off scot-free for even heinous crimes—if they can raise a convincing tear or two and have a defenseless (dead will do) nearby man to finger.

Both Herjury and Abuse Abuse exploit deep cultural biases that deem men to be mean and ugly and women to be pure and virtuous.

Sick of it yet? I know I am.

> "Emotional abuse has become a catch-all phrase used by some unprincipled women to justify themselves legally or morally in whatever they do vis-à-vis men. A man can defend himself against a spurious charge of physical abuse, to some degree, by demanding physical evidence. But emotional abuse can be anything and everything—how can any man effectively counter this charge?"
> —*columnist Glenn Sacks, July 2, 2002*

Choice for Men

> If the government has no right to force a woman into being a parent for nine months of pregnancy, why does the government have the right to force a man to be a parent for eighteen years of work and child support?

A man and woman who have sex and conceive a child are both responsible for that new life.

But the woman—and only the woman—can opt out of her responsibility by getting an abortion.

And the woman—and only the woman—can decide that the other person is going to be a parent against his wishes.

"During the 15 years I answered a Cleo advice column, I had many letters from women who were considering doing just that [tricking a man into fatherhood] and wrote seeking my approval for staging a 'supposed accident.'"
—*Bettina Arndt,* Sydney Morning Herald, *February 17, 2001*

Generally, the young, single mothers in London's public housing "estates" got pregnant on purpose. "There's huge peer pressure to have a baby," [Alan Craig, the director of the Mayflower Family Centre] says. "They want something to love. All their friends have babies; you see them pushing their prams with the babies dressed to the nines. They all want this toy, this doll."
derived from The Sunday Times *(London), September 3, 2000*

Choice for Men would allow a man to have a paper abortion: nobody dies, but the man is allowed to terminate all legal connections to the child.

But some people don't even want to allow you to have the benefit of Choice for children that aren't even yours!

> "The truth shall set you free."
> So we certainly can't let men know the truth!
>
> **(Feminacentrism seems to be in some people's DNA.)**
>
> **A disturbing variation on the old game "Mother May I?"**
>
> The British government's Human Genetics Commission has proposed a law, which government officials are expected to enact, to make it illegal for suspicious fathers to get DNA paternity tests without the mother's consent. One of the reasons: when a mother's lie is discovered things become "terribly difficult" for her. Officials in Australia, including the chief judge of the Family Court, have proposed similar restraints on men and fathers in their country.
>
> *derived from the Sunday Telegraph (London), May 19, 2002*
> *and the Melbourne Age (Australia), May 26, 2002*

Suicide

➤ If our lives are so wonderful and women's are so full of oppression and degradation, why do we commit suicide 4.5 times more often than girls and women do?

> The male-female suicide ratio is bad and getting worse. For 15-to-24-year-olds, the ratio in 1933 was 1.54 to 1. In 1971 it was 3.0 to 1. In 1995 it was 6.1 to 1.
> *derived from the US National Center for Health Statistics Centers for Disease Control*

> Since the mid-1970s the suicide rate involving Australian men between the ages of 20 and 39 has increased by 93 percent, growing by 18.5 per cent in just the past two years.
> *derived from* The Age, *Melbourne, October 17, 2000*

➤ Sure, more women than men "attempt" suicide, but if they "fail" so often we have to conclude either that they're incompetent… or they didn't really mean to "succeed."

> "The great bulk of non-fatal [suicide] attempts, which is to say the great bulk of female attempts, were very ambivalent about killing themselves. Men, generally, don't attempt suicide unless they are completely devoid of hope."
> —*Dr. David Clark, Director of the Center for Suicide Research past president of the American Association of Suicidology, in an interview with Jack Kammer, August 1992*

> "Call your mother, Gigi! Liane d'Exelmans has committed suicide."
> The child replied with a long drawn-out "Oooh!" and asked, "Is she dead?"
> "Of course not. She knows what she's about."
> —*from the French novel* Gigi *by Colette translated by Roger Senhouse*

In southern California in the late 1970s I was an Emergency Medical Technician working for an ambulance company. One day my partner and I got a call for a possible suicide. We arrived to find a 30-ish woman on the phone, pacing in the kitchen, sobbing to her girlfriend. She had taken a dozen aspirin. We walked her to the ambulance and she rode sitting up to the hospital emergency room. The very next call was another possible suicide. My unit was the first on the scene. We entered a dark apartment and found a large male form slumped backward across a bed. Touching the man's carotid artery to check for a pulse, I squeezed blood from his neck and saw it spilling from his mouth. He had blown his brains out.

It seems a most horrible and insensitive kind of irony that feminacentrists insist on pointing out that women "attempt suicide" more often than men do.

> **Blindness in Reporting Suicide**
>
> In a story about a rash of suicides at the University of Maryland, the *Washington Post* on July 16, 1992 reported that "six of the eight suicides were upperclass or graduate students," that "six of the eight suicides occurred this spring" and that "none of the suicides appeared to be related."
>
> They never reported that six of the eight victims were male.
>
> It seems unlikely that if six of the eight victims were female the *Post* would be oblivious to gender, especially if the gender factor were as startling for women as it is for men.
>
> • • •
>
> In covering a rash of youth suicides in South Boston, NBC News on May 6, 1997 never mentioned that all the victims were male. Neither did NPR's "Weekend All Things Considered," covering the same story on June 15, 1997.

➤ Why do we ignore the gender component of suicide? Because it would force us to acknowledge that this is not a man's world, and would require some changes our society would find difficult, inconvenient and threatening.

Saying What We Want to Say When and How We Want to Say It

I grew up believing that whenever any of my parents' friends got a divorce, it was always the man's fault. That made me feel bad about men… until I realized that it was only the women who were talking about fault.

It is "unchivalrous" for a man to discuss intimate details of his relationships with women. But no such rule restricts what women feel entitled to say about us.

> "Why do you feel you have to turn everything into a story?" So Nora told her why: "Because if I tell the story, I control the version."
>
> —*Nora Ephron in* Heartburn, *a semi-fictional novel of her failed marriage to journalist Carl Bernstein*

Imagine forty years ago that a black man is shot by a white police officer in a segregated American town. Imagine that the local newspaper story about the incident quotes only the police officer about what happened and why it happened, calling it an "ordeal" for the policeman and referring only to the black man as "the suspect," "the Negro" or "the perpetrator." Imagine that the Black paper in town is small and weak and published only irregularly and that it doesn't even mention the shooting because all of the Black witnesses are afraid to talk about it. What would that tell you about the relative power of whites and blacks in this town? Then what can we learn about the relative power of men and women in our society when only women are talking freely and unabashedly about what happens between them and us?

➢ One of the reasons we don't talk is that women don't listen.

"As listeners, wives tended to display more negative nonverbal behavior than their husbands. Wives were negative listeners 11% of the time, compared to their husbands' 3%."

"Negative face cues" include "frown, sneer, fear, crying, angry face or disgust."

"Negative voice cues" are "cold, tense, fearful, impatient, whining, sarcastic, blaming, angry, hurt, mocking or depressed."

"Negative body position cues" are "arms akimbo (with hands on hip), tense neck or hands, inattentive, pointing, jabbing or slicing with hand."

—*Clifford I. Notarius and Jennifer S. Johnson;* Journal of Marriage and the Family, *1982*

"Men like to please women and gain their approval, so they give their power away. Men are incredibly afraid of women; they have tremendous fear of women if they feel that the woman is going to criticize them. Frequently when he expresses himself, she says, 'Oh, don't be so ridiculous; I can't believe you're saying that!' or 'Why don't you ever talk about your feelings?' Then when the guy talks about his feelings, she'll often say, 'That's stupid!' or 'You can't really feel that way!' So the way he sees it is never right. And so the guy shuts down, and he refuses to talk. That's what I see in my practice over and over. The guy wonders, 'Why should I open my mouth, when every time I do, she tells me it's wrong?'"

—*therapist Laurie Ingraham*
in Good Will Toward Men *by Jack Kammer*

➤ One of the reasons we don't talk is that we've learned that women would rather not hear what we really have to say.

"[During] a seminar I did with black men and women… the men decided they wanted to express to the women some things that they had never had a chance to say… So the men started expressing their pain and disappointment. They started expressing how they feel about not being accepted for who they are, for not having their struggle recognized, for having women respond to them in very self-centered ways where the women were only talking about what they needed, what they wanted. 'You want, want, want all the time. Can't you see that I'm working with very limited resources? I'm doing the best I can.'… And as they were in the midst of talking about that, the women lit into them. I mean they fired at them! The women started screaming and yelling at them, 'How dare they be so insensitive and uncaring!' and all the kinds of foul statements that can be made. And the men shut down. They shut down. They couldn't say another word."

—*Audrey Chapman, therapist and author of*
Getting Good Loving: How Black Men and Women Can Make Love Work, *in* Good Will Toward Men *by Jack Kammer*

➢ One of the most effective ways women keep us quiet is by subtly threatening us with words: misogynist, woman-hater, sexist, chauvinist, misfit, troublemaker, loser, weirdo, whiner, jerk.

> Newspaper columnist D.L. Stewart says that he told a good friend of his, a female police reporter, that he was writing a series of columns about workshops on Men's Issues at the University of Dayton. Her immediate reaction was, "Oh, what are you poor babies whining about now?"
> D.L. says he was astounded.
> Speechless.

➢ Did you ever notice that when we have opinions that women don't like, they're not called opinions, but "attitudes"?

The "Sensitive" Man

Being sensitive on women's command is merely taking insensitivity to a higher plane. We are already too sensitive for our own good in a culture that doesn't really care how we feel.

➤ It's a good news/bad news joke. The good news is that women want us to be more sensitive. The bad news is that they want us to be more sensitive to them.

If women think we're callous they need to recognize that calluses form to protect sensitive spots from repeated irritation. Our situation in life is like a pair of mass-produced boots that all men must wear. "Built for durability. Black only. One size fits all, no matter what you say."

➤ For men, calluses are indispensable equipment.

A Conversation Between a Woman and a Sensitive Man

The man: "Hi. Sure is a pretty night. I've never been on a cruise before. I only wish we weren't on the Titanic. I'm a very sensitive man and before you get into that lifeboat and leave me here to drown, I'd really like to share my feelings with you. I'm feeling very sad. I'm feeling like I'm really going to miss my wife and kids back in Kokomo. I'm feeling that we should flip a coin to see who gets the last seat in that lifeboat."

The woman: "Oh, that's so beautiful. I so much admire a man who's in touch with his feelings. Have a nice swim."

(What would happen on the Titanic today? According to the *Pittsburgh Tribune-Review*, May 3, 1998, the National Organization for Women has not considered that question. Would a childless female lawyer be saved while a father with three children back home would be left to die?)

➤ If we suddenly became more sensitive but nothing else changed in our lives, all we'd feel is more pain.

The Straightforward Man

One of the very most crippling limitations society places on us is in our freedom to talk about what's really going on in our lives. The fancy term for that is "to get in touch with your feelings." Or "expressing your emotions." (Notice how these things have come to sound "girly.")

But even though they sound "girly" they are the essence of staying happy and healthy—for us as much as for women. When you have a problem, you have a right to speak up about it, to get feedback from people you trust and to seek help in solving it. And if others are causing the problem or making it worse you have a right to say you would like them to stop. (Whether they actually should stop or whether they have a right to keep doing it is another matter. You won't—and probably shouldn't—always get your way. But if you don't speak up, you'll never get your way. You'll just become more and more unhappy and aggravated.)

Wanting to talk about something doesn't mean it's a "big deal" or you "can't handle it." It only means that something happened or is happening, it's on your mind and you think you'd like to take it out of its dark closet and put some sunshine on it. Hearing other people say, "Wow, that must have been awful" or "That must feel terrible" or "You must be really disappointed" or "I know exactly what you mean" or "That would have made me furious!" or "I'm glad you said something; I thought I was the only person who felt that way" can confirm for you and remind you that you are perfectly normal for feeling the way you feel. One of the worst things about keeping an unpleasant feeling clamped inside is that it allows you to get infected with a nagging doubt that maybe what is wrong is all your fault and you are therefore completely unworthy and unlovable—a loser, a whiner, not a "real" man.

Often you'll be afraid you're making a mountain out of a molehill. We hate being told that we're "whining." But here's a good test. If what's on your mind is causing you discomfort when it would normally have been forgotten, it's not important whether it's big or little. What's important is how it still hurts you. Your feelings are like your eyes; they're important and delicate. Would you ignore a speck of grit in your eye just because it's small, because "it's no big deal"?

Your emotions are the spark plugs of your personality. Don't ever let anyone disconnect or re-wire them. Don't ever let anyone take your ignition key.

Speak up when you have something to say. And although the truth doesn't have to be nice to be true, say it as nicely, as confidently and sincerely—as straightforwardly—as you can.

Listen to me. I know what I feel.

One of the best things that happens when you really accept and trust your feelings is that they can give you a sense of direction. They help you know which way is up. They can give you backbone. As long as you're being honest, you are never wrong when you start your statements with "I feel…"

If you're in an argument you can reach down deep and say, "I understand what you're saying and I think I understand how you feel. But you need to listen to how I feel, too. My feelings are every bit as right and valid and worthy of respect and consideration as yours. You can roll your eyes if you want to. You can tell me I'm ridiculous. But this is how I feel. We can either keep talking or we can stop now. But I will not let you get away with acting like your feelings are automatically more important or more valid than mine."

Before I learned to insist on those ground rules, my disagreements with women would usually end with me feeling angry, frustrated and defeated, and not really knowing why. The reason, I now know, is that women are well-trained and well-versed in discussions of their feelings and they expect and even demand that their feelings be heard and respected. They're not so good at hearing and respecting ours. And we haven't been so good at demanding that we get a chance to put them on the table.

> "[T]he most powerful technique of all [in having an argument with a woman]: Tell her how you feel at the moment… 'Honey, I'm feeling really angry as I listen to you, because I feel I am being blamed for things that keep happening in our relationship. We had a similar misunderstanding last week and I felt blamed, and now it's happening again and I am feeling really pushed around.'… Often, men find it more difficult than women, because it requires you to reveal something of your feelings in a moment of emotional stress…. It's also difficult because you are feeling some emotion and you need to step back and see exactly how you feel and report it."
> —*Michael Crichton,* Playboy, *December 1991*

I am in touch with my feelings.
And they want to stay out of touch with you!

If you're feeling that you don't want to talk about your feelings, trust your feelings and don't talk. You have a right to feel safe before anyone can expect you to "open up."

You don't absolutely have to talk about your feelings to feel them. You don't have to "share" them to be "in touch" with them. When you're with a good friend, when you feel really safe, it can be good to express them. But if the person you're talking with isn't going to respect your feelings, you'll be better off keeping them to yourself. Lots of people, after all, don't respect our feelings; lots of people don't even think we have any feelings at all.

And some people want to hear about our feelings only so they can shame and manipulate us with them.

It's Okay. Really.

On the other hand, it can sometimes be good when you don't feel a need to talk about your feelings. For instance, if someone has hurt you and you know it was an accident and you know the other person will never do the hurtful thing or anything like it ever again, it can be a real expression of your strength and love to be able to process the hurt internally without having to "talk it out" and making the other person squarely face his or her mistake. Just forgive her.

But the choice and the decision should always be yours. If you think it will help you to talk, do it. If you're okay on your own—really okay, not just faking it behind some macho mask—then forget about it. Talking about feelings isn't always the best way to deal with them.

It can be a great sign of maturity that you can absorb some pain and problems without a hitch. But in your effort to "be a man" you need to remember that being a man also requires you to have and maintain your Integrity, to demand that the people in your life must treat you with dignity and respect—even though occasionally, no matter what, bad things will happen.

Twenty-one Points for Women Who Want Their Men to "Open Up"[†]

A perfectly valid word for an exchange of thoughts and feelings is "intercourse." There's a good reason for this. For every complaint that women have about how we try to get sex from them, we can make a similar point about how women try to get emotion from us.

1. Don't just snap your fingers and say, "Open up."

2. Though you may feel a strong urge to "do it," men are different. Intercourse does not always have to be in and out, back and forth. Men value and enjoy non-verbal intercourse, like being understood and accepted for what they are, not what they say.

3. You can't force intercourse and expect your man to enjoy it. You might force him to fake an understanding just to get it over with.

[†] I wrote this piece in 1987 on assignment for Jan Warrington, then features editor of the *Baltimore Sun*. She had asked for a male response to a much-publicized new book by Shere Hite which harped on women's old complaint that men don't express enough emotion. She killed the article because, she said, it has "an undercurrent of sarcasm and anger toward women." [God forbid!]

4. Men will not hop into emotional intimacy with just anyone. Men know that women are always ready to get into somebody's head. You must convince him that he is not just another piece of mind.

5. You should let him be on top sometimes. Men are tired of being in the inferior position, especially in hot and passionate intercourse.

6. Don't perform tricks that make him feel inadequate. Remember that you have been raised with more skill in intercourse than he has.

7. Men were taught that only women are supposed to enjoy intercourse. Help him not to feel guilty and weird for doing it.

8. Let him take control sometimes. Don't insist on controlling whose needs must be met when.

9. Don't talk and tell. Don't get him to "put out" and then rush to your women friends with the intimate details.

10. If your thrusting and probing hurts him, stop immediately. Don't assume that he'll start to like it just because you do.

11. Allow him to initiate. Don't hit on him with so many requests for intercourse that he never feels the urge to start intercourse at his own pace, according to his own needs.

12. Men are often shy and insecure about their flaws and blemishes, about whether you will find them attractive. Don't expect your man to show you everything right away.

13. Remember that good intercourse is not a wrestling match. There should be no winner and no loser.

14. Respect your lover as an equal partner. You don't own him; he does not exist for the sole purpose of providing your pleasure.

15. If you have ever abused him during intercourse, understand that it may take a long, long time for your man to open up to you again.

16. Keep in mind that men's and women's rhythms are different. Don't get angry if his needs don't coincide with yours.

17. If you simply want to release tension, let him know. Don't pretend that you're doing it for him. Men often resist intercourse if they feel pressured about "getting into it."

18. There is no such thing as the ideal lover. Don't try to make your partner into something he isn't. Accept your man as he is.

19. Foreplay is essential; gentle stroking of the ego can help. If you encounter a ravenous ego, remember it is ravenous not because it gets too much healthy attention, but because it gets too little.

20. Don't get hung up on achieving simultaneous understanding. Men's understandings take longer, but they are usually more intense.

21. Respect him in the morning.

> Writer Daphne Patai wonders what it would be like if we started alleging "emotional harassment" against women who demand that we "share" our emotions.

Here's a new rule. We get to talk and say what's on our minds without fear of being attacked or ridiculed. Women get to listen without fear that just listening signifies any acceptance whatsoever of what we're saying. And we've got lots to say.

We need to start saying it.

ENDING OUR COLLUSION IN WOMEN'S UNFAIRNESS

We collude in the restrictions, the limited life options, that women often want and depend on us to accept. Like soldiers trained to salute sharply and say "Yes, ma'am!" we meekly accept our assignments, our orders, our inability to explore the full range of options that women take for granted.

Our collusion is understandable since women have so much power and we are loathe to displease them, but we need at least to recognize our role in allowing the situation to persist.

In fact, in some ways we're even rougher on ourselves than women are. It often happens that a group that's down feels the need to keep its members in line, whether to protect them from the adverse consequences of bucking authority and stepping outside the norm or to play out angry, resentful feelings that rigidly say "If it's bad enough for me, it's bad enough for you."

> **A poll Marilyn Vos Savant conducted in January 2000
> with the readers of her column in Parade Magazine
> Answers from 7,758 readers**
>
> 1. Should we teach our daughters they have a choice between having a career and staying at home?
>   - 83% of the men said yes; 17% said no.
>   - 77% of the women said yes; 23% said no.
> 2. Should we teach our sons they have a choice between having a career and staying at home?
>   - 28% of the men said yes; 72% said no.
>   - 40% of the women said yes; 60% said no.

We need to acknowledge, not resentfully but with determination, that in some ways it was and is bad for us. Although I know of no study that has attempted to measure it, it seems clear enough that men's lives are more likely than women's to be joyless. I doubt, for instance, that it was a woman who coined the hyper-cynical saying, "Life's a bitch and then you die."

And juvenile delinquency, vandalism and other anti-social behaviors are often ways for boys to express their disgust with adult society, especially with us adult men for allowing ourselves to be in our restricted, difficult situation and expecting them to accept it as docilely as we did.

> "Over the years, countless troubled [boys] have crossed into my office—slouching, 'underachieving' boys whose parents are at their wits' end. I often frame them in my mind as little protesters, sit-down strikers refusing to march off into the state of alienation we call manhood. If the choice is between success and connection, many boys simply refuse to play. We usually call these boys delinquents."
> —*therapist Terrence Real in his 1997 book* I Don't Want to Talk About It: Overcoming the Secret Legacy of Male Depression

There is another powerful force at work that induces and even forces us into colluding in the system that allows us so few options for pursuing happiness.

Think back to the beginning of this book where the *coup de grace* on the woman's faxed copy of The Rules was "The male who doesn't abide by The Rules lacks backbone and is a wimp." In other words, play according to our rules or we'll kick you where it hurts the most. We'll accuse you of not being manly. We'll spread the word that you're a wuss. We'll disgrace and shame you.

What a clever way to keep us under control, to keep us stuck right where we've always been! We're deathly afraid of not being seen as manly. It is, in fact, an obsession. A search of the Nexis online electronic database on March 26, 2001 turned up 369 major articles in which the word "prove" was within three words of the words "manhood" or "masculinity." When the search was switched to "womanhood" or "femininity" there were only 28 articles. Similarly, the Yahoo Internet search engine produced 23,720 hits that had something to do with proving masculinity, but only 5,330 concerned in some way with proving femininity.

Throughout history we have severely and unnecessarily inconvenienced and limited ourselves for fear of being seen as "effeminate." We've passed up on things we wanted to do. We've endured more inconvenience and hardship and unhappiness than we needed to. Take a look at some of the things we now use every day, take for granted and even in some cases love, things that were once "considered effeminate."

In American football, the forward pass was invented precisely because the original running game of football, with its infamous flying wedge, was getting too rough and dangerous. The forward pass was intended to make the game safer but some "purists" derided it as "unmanly."[5] We can see remnants of that thinking even today in Aussie Rules Football, in which "throwing the ball results in a free kick to the other team and taunts of

---

[5] "Football History Was Made Here at SLU," St. Louis University. www.slu.edu/publications/gc/v6-6/news_24.shtml; "131 Years of Princeton Football, Princeton University. <www.princeton.edu/football/history.htm>

'Sheila' from the crowd."[6] Though some American football fans thought the forward pass would ruin the game, "public interest in football soared. A game that had been predicated to a great extent on brute strength became a game of position, balance, speed, mobility and leverage. It still paid to be strong, but now you had to be more than strong."[7]

When the helmet first showed up on football fields, Pudge Heffelfinger, Yale's three-time All American from 1889-1891 said, "None of that sissy stuff for me."[8]

In 1611 Thomas Coryat, an Englishman, saw forks being used in Italy. When he brought them back to England, he was widely ridiculed for feminine airs.[9]

Frederick William, an 18th-century Prussian king and father of Frederick the Great, beat his son for wearing gloves in cold weather because it was "an effeminate behavior, worthy only of Frenchmen."[10]

Wristwatches at first were considered effeminate because "real men" carried pocket

---

[6] *The (Official) Idiot's Guide to Aussie Rules Football*
[7] "75 Years Ago: Late Autumn/Early Winter 1926" by Maurice Telleen, *The Draft Horse Journal* (Winter 2000-2001)
[8] "American Football" by Bruce K. Stewart in *American History*, November 1995
[9] Ludwig von Mises Institute. <www.mises.org/efandi/ch5.asp>
[10] "Frederick the Great (1712-1786)" by Mary Lou Derksen. <www.suite101.com/article.cfm/childhoods_famous_people/22805>

watches.[11]

In ancient Greece, using hot water was considered effeminate; a man's bath typically was a quick bucket of cold water dumped on his head.[12]

Up through the Civil War, cigarettes were considered unmanly because men smoked only pipes and cigars.[13] The derogatory term "fag" for homosexual male might be related to the fact that gay men were among the first to adopt cigarettes, which in Britain were and still are called "fags."[14]

Umbrellas[15], drinking from a cup[16], long sleeves[17] and open collars revealing the chest[18] all were deemed unmanly as well.

---

[11] Bob Brink. "The Art and History of Collectible Watches," *Palm Beach Illustrated Magazine*, May 2000; de Burton, Simon. "Tough, Rugged and Accurate." *The Financial Times*, June 08, 2007; The Timepiece Store, "The History of Wrist Watches," December 17, 2008.

[12] "The History of Plumbing." www.theplumber.com/greek.html; *Dictionary of Greek and Roman Antiquities*, William Smith (ed.) (1870). p. 184

[13] "Empires of Industry," The History Channel. "Tips for Tobacco Users" [for Civil War Re-enactors]. <www.shasta.com/suesgoodco/newcivilians/advice/tobacco.htm>

[14] *Cassell's Dictionary of Slang*, Jonathon Green, London: Weidenfeld & Nicolson (2005), p. 484

[15] "Ask the Globe," *The Boston Globe*, March 20, 1991. p. 82

[16] *Surgeon Grow: An American in the Russian Fighting*, Malcolm C. Grow (1918). New York: Frederick A. Stokes. <www.vlib.us/medical/russdoc/Rdoc05.htm>

[17] University of Chicago class notes. <penelope.uchicago.edu/ross/ross216.html>

[18] Hurstwic, a living history society in New England. <www.valhs.org/history/articles/daily_living/text/clothing.htm>

Pretty ridiculous, isn't it? Fortunately, our fear of being associated with good things that somehow get labeled unmanly is eventually overruled by good sense.

So here's a prediction: pretty soon hardly any man will feel the least bit wimpish, unmanly or otherwise abnormal for speaking up about the ways sexism affects us. We'll look back and see that standing up for ourselves and asserting our reasonable rights to what we want and need is perfectly acceptable and even expected masculine behavior. And we'll wonder how we ever believed anything else, even though some women—and some forkophobic henchmen, too, no doubt—will try to shame us with nonsensical suggestions that "real" men let women make the rules about how they should think and feel and act.

The insinuation that we're wimps if we don't follow the feminacentrist prescription of what's manly is old and tired technology. Let's get over it. Let's enjoy happier, fuller lives. Let's demand that women treat us more fairly, sharing the options they'd prefer to keep all for themselves.

"Considered Effeminate"
would be a great name for a rock band.

Statistics, "Studies," "Reports" and Other Smokescreens

In the Womenfirsters' campaign to get Whatever Women Want, there are lies, damn lies and femstats. The term "femstat" was coined by Asa Baber in his column in the April 1990 issue of *Playboy* magazine: "Feminist statistics, often gathered in a strange and cavalier fashion and quoted liberally; statistics that are used to supposedly prove the unequal status of women and the triumph of men."

> "No one cares what the real numbers are. They just want to make political statements."
>
> —Kathryn Newcomer
> *professor of statistics and public policy at George Washington University*
> *in Insight magazine*
> *commenting on widely published rape statistics*

> The director of the UCLA Center for Women and Men told a reporter from the student newspaper that the "one-in-four" rape statistic was accurate and in fact had been published by the FBI and the American Medical Association on their websites. But when she was told by another journalist that this was untrue, she said, "The statistics don't really matter that much in the big picture. We're just trying to focus on the real issue here, to debate about civil rights, not bicker about numbers."
> *derived from National Review Online, May 18, 2001*

Don't fall into the trap of arguing over femstats. You'll simply be outgunned. Millions of dollars of government and foundation money each year fund "advocacy research"—bogus and biased PR spinning machines masquerading as "studies" and "surveys." Even if the studies are valid, they're often wildly distorted, misinterpreted and misquoted.

> "Bad statistics are harder to kill than vampires."
> —*Joel Best, author of the 2001 book* Damned Lies and Statistics: Untangling Numbers From the Media, Politicians and Activists, New York Times, *May 26, 2001*

> "When I inquired of Miss Hoeffler how she had arrived at the 40 per cent depression figure in the face of the finding that women were enjoying life most of the time, she candidly told me she was very concerned that the Harris study not be just another study reflecting 'white male norms' of research, adding that... she was doing her best to counter 'phallocentric bias.' I was not surprised to find that she had specialized in feminist theory at Hunter College. According to one Washington, D.C., researcher to whom I recently spoke: 'Under Secretary Shalala, Health and Human Services has been mobilized as the research and policy arm of the feminist movement.'"
>
> —*Christina Hoff Sommers, Ph.D., author of* Who Stole Feminism; *in the* National Review, *September 2, 1996*

"Data Rape"

Forcing statistics and other data to bend and yield to the will of someone more interested in her own satisfaction and gratification than in fairness and respect for truth. (Term coined by Lindsay Jackel of Melbourne, Australia.)

Here is an example of how reckless femstats can be. A study of violence—all violence, not just domestic violence—was conducted in a poor, inner city Philadelphia neighborhood. Twelve percent of the perpetrators of injury to women were male domestic partners. But when Surgeon General Antonia Novello said correctly that "one study found violence [all violence, not just domestic violence] to be… the leading cause of injury to women ages 15 through 44 years," it was seized upon and distorted by women's activists. A domestic violence pamphlet said "findings by the Surgeon General reveal that domestic violence is the leading cause of injury to women between ages 15 and 44, more common than automobile accidents, muggings and cancer combined." The femstat was then picked up in an editorially shoddy *Newsweek* article, and now it is widely quoted in "everyone knows" tones.

> "When it comes to gender issues, journalists generally have suspended all their usual skepticism… We accept at face value whatever women's groups say. Why? Because women have sold themselves to us as an oppressed group and any oppressed group gets a free ride in the press… I don't blame feminists for telling us half-truths and sometimes even complete fabrications. I do blame my colleagues in the press for forgetting their skepticism."
>
> —*former CBS News Correspondent Bernard Goldberg interviewed by Jack Kammer in Quill: The Magazine for Journalists, May 1992*

We've talked about the Super Bowl domestic violence femstat (see page 38). Other examples of femstats that pheminism often uses to berate us:

- men's standard of living goes up after divorce[i]
- one out of four college women will be victims of rape or attempted rape[ii].

When these numbers are dropped on you, you can use two tactics. The first is to challenge their authenticity by saying something like this:

"Would you believe a 'study' by an 'expert' at an economic 'institute' funded by General Motors that said auto makers deserved a tax subsidy? Then why do you expect me to believe the biased, self-serving and unscientific numbers pheminism generates to support its agenda?"

Or this:

"That pseudo-study was done by a Womenfirst zealot who used a small, self-selected group of people to get the result she wanted. It's SLOP[19]. It's bogus."

---

[i] the widely quoted work of Lenore Weitzman has been debunked by peer review and revelations of serious statistical and methodological errors; Weitzman herself was finally forced to admit the errors, blaming them on a computer problem. See *American Sociological Review*, June 1996. See also Cathy Young's 1999 book *Ceasefire!*.

[ii] the widely quoted work of Mary Koss has been debunked by revelations of her ludicrously broad definitions of rape; see Christina Hoff Sommers' 1994 book *Who Stole Feminism?*.

[19] Self-selected Listener Opinion Polls. Bogus "studies" in which responses come from people motivated to respond to a particular questionnaire, not from a scientifically representative sample.

Or this:

"I'd like to see the original study. Pheminism and the media have a poor record when it comes to keeping statistics on gender issues straight."

Or this:

"How did they define… ?"

> "The [one-in-four rape] figure was based on spurious research, which included a question using the following definition of rape: 'Have you had sexual intercourse when you didn't want to because a man gave you alcohol or drugs?' Hmmmm. I can count on two hands, no toes, the number of women who would answer 'no' to this question. How about this as an answer: 'Yes, we drank a few beers and I wasn't in the mood, but I did it anyway.'"
>
> —*columnist Kathleen Parker, townhall.com, May 13, 2002*

The second tactic involves a conceptual attack on the bogus Womenfirst claim. For instance:

When she says	You say
Women make 59 cents for every dollar earned by men.	If women really made 59 cents on the dollar for the same work as men, what business could compete by hiring any men at all?[†]
95% of all domestic violence is committed by men against women.	That's based on police reports. Men are embarrassed to report being pounded on by their wives.
40% of child support is never paid; this shows that men are irresponsible and don't care about their kids.	How many women would obey court orders to continue cooking and cleaning for their husbands after they're divorced, especially if he took the kids away from her? Besides, women's compliance with child support orders is much worse than men's.

[†] Thanks to Warren Farrell, Ph.D., author of *Women Can't Hear What Men Don't Say*.

If and when you get to the point where you need your own hard numbers and statistics to use in discussions of gender issues, these three books will serve you well:
- *Women Can't Hear What Men Don't Say* by Warren Farrell (October 1999)
- *Ceasefire: Why Women and Men Must Join Forces to Achieve True Equality* by Cathy Young (February 1999)
- *Who Stole Feminism? How Women Have Betrayed Women* by Christina Hoff Sommers (May 1994)

For an up-to-date listing of other good sources of ideas and information, see "Links and Other Resources" at www.RulyMob.com. I will maintain an up-to-date listing of the most noteworthy sites to visit or books to read. The list will necessarily be brief, subjective and incomplete, but it will be a good starting place if you want to read more or get involved in advocacy and activism on behalf of fairness to men.

LEXICON

> "The notion of giving something a name is the vastest generative idea that was ever conceived."
>
> —*Suzanne K. Langer*
> *as quoted by Gloria Steinem in* Revolution from Within.

Daffynition — A definition of a topic of "research" that has been so flattened and cheapened as to be ludicrous. For instance, including "he failed to pay you compliments" as a definition of abuse.

Data Rape — Forcing statistics and other data to bend and yield to the will of someone more interested in her own satisfaction and gratification than in fairness and respect for truth.

Front Man — A man occupying an illusory position of "male power" who is actually operating under the control and bidding of women and pheminist/chivalrous/chauvinist ideology.

Feminacentrism — The bias of looking at all problems exclusively from women's perspective, or for the purpose of seeing how women are affected. Feminacentrism is blind to the problems men face.

Femstats	Bogus pheminist statistics, recklessly and wantonly promulgated by pheminists; often gullibly and sloppily repeated by the media
Herjury	False allegations of sexual misconduct leveled against a man by a woman
Lace Curtain	The refusal of media gatekeepers to acknowledge or allow publication of ideas and data that challenge pheminist ideology and femstats; the reason this book is self-published.
Masculism	The belief that achieving fairness and equity between the sexes requires addressing sexism against men as well as against women.
Misandry	Unreasoning, reflexive hatred, fear or distrust of men.
NOWWW	The National Organization for Whatever Women Want; American culture since the 1970s.
Pheminism	A term combining "phony" and "feminism" to denote the wrongheaded idea that "equal rights for women" is the same thing as "more and special rights for women."
Womenfirster	A person motivated by a primary and overriding concern for women's interests even when they come at the expense of fairness to men and the common good.

Conclusion

If anything in this book rings true for you, you can be sure you're not imagining things. You can put aside your haunting suspicion that because you think some things are pretty unfair for men you must have a "personal problem."[20] You're not a malcontent, a jerk, a loser, a Neanderthal, a woman-hater or a weirdo. The fact that you have been made to feel that way is testimony to the power and effectiveness of the old advice, "Divide and conquer." As men we've been worse than divided. We've been isolated and alienated—not only from each other, but even from our own selves and from our own belief in what we see and experience.

I hope you're saying to yourself, "Okay. So now what?"

First, the good news: for starters, all you have to do is talk about it.

Now, the bad news: you have to talk about it. A lot. As much as you can. Even when you're afraid.

Ask other men if they've ever thought about these things. Tell them you've read this book. Give them a copy. See what they have to say. You'll be surprised at how much agreement you'll find once you overcome your fear that you're alone in what you think.

---

[20] The very most common remark from readers of the first edition of *If Men Have...* has been some variation of "Thank God I found your book. I thought I was the only man in the world who was thinking these things. I was afraid I was going crazy."

And don't be afraid to speak up just because women are around. You'll find that lots of women will agree and have been wondering why we put up with what we put up with. And tell the ones who disagree that they ought to read this book—if they can open their minds a little.

The goal right now is just to make it natural and comfortable for men to speak openly and forthrightly about the changes we want and need in our lives.

Nothing good can happen until we achieve that. Everything good can happen afterward.

ABOUT THE AUTHOR

Jack Kammer is pretty much a regular fellow who believes that we should have as much happiness, joy, freedom, fairness and dignity in our lives as women have in theirs.

[21] Photograph by Lisa Strickland

Made in the USA
Lexington, KY
28 May 2011